Lecture Notes in Computer Science 7488

Commenced Publication in 1973
Founding and Former Series Editors:
Gerhard Goos, Juris Hartmanis, and Jan van Leeuwen

Tiziana Catarci Pamela Forner
Djoerd Hiemstra Anselmo Peñas
Giuseppe Santucci (Eds.)

Information Access Evaluation

Multilinguality, Multimodality,
and Visual Analytics

Third International Conference
of the CLEF Initiative, CLEF 2012
Rome, Italy, September 17-20, 2012
Proceedings

 Springer

Volume Editors

Tiziana Catarci
Giuseppe Santucci
Sapienza University of Rome, Dept. of Computer, Control and Management
Engeneering Antonio Ruberti
Via Ariosto 25, 00185 Rome, Italy
E-mail: {catarci, santucci}@dis.uniroma1.it

Pamela Forner
Center for the Evaluation of Language and Communication Technologies (CELCT)
Via alla Cascata 56/c, 38123 Povo, TN, Italy
E-mail: forner@celct.it

Djoerd Hiemstra
University of Twente, Dept. of Computer Science, Database Group
PO Box 217, 7500 AE Enschede, The Netherlands
E-mail: hiemstra@cs.utwente.nl

Anselmo Peñas
UNED Natural Language Processing and Information Retrieval Research Group
E.T.S.I. Informática de la UNED
c/ Juan del Rosal 16, 28040 Madrid, Spain
E-mail: anselmo@lsi.uned.es

ISSN 0302-9743   e-ISSN 1611-3349
ISBN 978-3-642-33246-3   e-ISBN 978-3-642-33247-0
DOI 10.1007/978-3-642-33247-0
Springer Heidelberg Dordrecht London New York

Library of Congress Control Number: 2012946265

CR Subject Classification (1998): I.7, I.2.7, H.3.1, H.3.3, H.3.7, H.4.1, H.5.3, H.2.8,
I.1.3

LNCS Sublibrary: SL 3 – Information Systems and Application, incl. Internet/Web
and HCI

Typesetting: Camera-ready by author, data conversion by Scientific Publishing Services, Chennai, India

Printed on acid-free paper

Springer is part of Springer Science+Business Media (www.springer.com)

Preface

Since 2000 the Cross-Language Evaluation Forum (CLEF) has played a leading role in stimulating research and innovation in a wide range of key areas in the domain of multimodal and multilingual information access. Through the years, CLEF has promoted the study and implementation of evaluation methodologies for diverse tasks, resulting in the creation of a broad, strong, and multidisciplinary research community.

Until 2010, the outcomes of experiments carried out under the CLEF umbrella were presented and discussed at annual workshops in conjunction with the European Conference for Digital Libraries. CLEF 2010 represented a radical departure from this "classic" CLEF format. While preserving CLEF's traditional core goals, namely, benchmarking activities carried in various tracks, we complemented these activities with a peer-reviewed conference component aimed at advancing research in the evaluation of complex information access systems in different languages and modalities.

CLEF 2011 and CLEF 2012 continued to implement this format, with keynotes, contributed papers, lab sessions, poster sessions, reporting of other benchmarking initiatives and, for the first time this year, an evaluation clinic session where people with retrieval evaluation problems of some kind would be able to talk to evaluation experts and get methodological advice, new ideas, pointers to related problems, available solutions, etc.

This year, the papers accepted for the conference included research on information access and evaluation initiatives, methodologies, and infrastructures. Two keynote speakers highlighted important issues related to our field. Peter Clark (Vulcan Inc.) presented a case of innovation turned into a company product that allows users not only to read and browse a textbook, but also to ask questions and get reasoned or retrieved answers back, explore the material through semantic connections, and receive suggestions of useful questions to ask. Tobias Schreck (University of Konstanz), on the other hand, showed current approaches, applications, and challenges for the application of visual analytics in document repositories.

CLEF 2012 featured seven benchmarking activities: RepLab, INEX, QA4MRE, CLEF-IP, ImageCLEF, PAN, and CHiC. In parallel, the CLEFeHealth workshop was hosted, dealing with cross-language evaluation of methods, applications, and resources for eHealth document analysis with a focus on written and spoken natural-language processing.

All the experiments carried out by systems during the evaluation campaigns are described in a separate publication, namely, the Working Notes, distributed during CLEF 2012 and available on-line.

The success of CLEF 2012 would not have been possible without the invaluable contributions of all the members of the Program Committee, Organizing Committee, students and volunteers that supported the conference in its various stages. We would like to express also our gratitude to the sponsoring organizations for their significant and timely support. These proceedings were prepared with the assistance of the Center for the Evaluation of Language and Communication Technologies (CELCT), Trento, Italy.

July 2012

Tiziana Catarci
Pamela Forner
Djoerd Hiemstra
Anselmo Peñas
Giuseppe Santucci

Organization

CLEF 2012 was organized by Sapienza University of Rome, Italy.

General Chairs

Tiziana Catarci   Sapienza University of Rome, Italy
Djoerd Hiemstra   University of Twente, The Netherlands

Program Chairs

Anselmo Peñas   National Distance Learning University, Spain
Giuseppe Santucci   Sapienza University of Rome, Italy

Evaluation Labs Chairs

Jussi Karlgren   Swedish Institute of Computer Science, Sweden
Christa Womser-Hacker   University of Hildesheim, Germany

Resource Chair

Khalid Choukri   Evaluations and Language Resources Distribution
                               Agency (ELDA), France

Organization Chair

Emanuele Pianta   Center for the Evaluation of Language and
                               Communication Technologies (CELCT), Italy

Organizing Committee

Sapienza University of Rome, Italy:

Carola Aiello
Giuseppe Santucci

Consulta Umbria Congressi, Perugia, Italy

Center for the Evaluation of Language and Communication Technologies (CELCT), Italy:

Pamela Forner
Giovanni Moretti

Program Committee

Alexandra Balahur	Joint Research Centre - JRC - European Commission, Italy
Yassine Benajiba	Philips, USA
Khalid Choukri	Evaluations and Language Resources Distribution Agency (ELDA), France
Walter Daelemans	University of Antwerp, Belgium
Nicola Ferro	University of Padua, Italy
Norbert Fuhr	University of Duisburg, Germany
Julio Gonzalo	National Distance Learning University, Spain
Donna Harman	National Institute of Standard and Technology, USA
Gareth Jones	Dublin City University, Ireland
Noriko Kando	National Institute of Informatics, Japan
Evangelos Kanoulas	Google, Switzerland
Bernardo Magnini	Fondazione Bruno Kessler, Italy
Prasenjit Majumder	Dhirubhai Ambani Institute of Information and Communication Technology, India
Thomas Mandl	University of Hildesheim, Germany
Paul McNamee	Johns Hopkins University, USA
Manuel Montes-y-Gómez	National Institute of Astrophysics, Optics and Electronics, Mexico
Henning Müller	University of Applied Sciences Western Switzerland, Switzerland
Jian-Yun Nie	University of Montreal, Canada
Carol Peters	ISTI CNR Pisa, Italy
Vivien Petras	Humboldt University, Germany
Álvaro Rodrigo	National Distance Learning University, Spain
Paolo Rosso	Universitat Politècnica de València, Spain
Tobias Schreck	University of Konstanz, Germany
José Luis Vicedo	University of Alicante, Spain
Christa Womser-Hacker	University of Hildesheim, Germany

Sponsoring Institutions   .

CLEF 2012 benefited from the support of the following organizations:

Gold Sponsors

   ELIAS

   PROMISE Network of Excellence

Sapienza University of Rome

Silver Sponsors

   European Science Foundation

   Quaero

From Information Retrieval to Knowledgeable Machines

Peter Clark

Vulcan Inc.,
505 Fifth Ave South, Suite 900,
Seattle, WA, 98104
peterc@vulcan.com

Abstract. Ultimately we would like our machines to not only search and retrieve information, but also have some "understanding" of the material that they are manipulating so that they can better meet the user's needs. In this talk, I will present our work in Project Halo to create an (iPad hosted) "knowledgeable biology textbook", called Inquire. Inquire includes a formal, hand-crafted knowledge base encoding some of the book's content, being augmented (this year) with capabilities for textual entailment and question-answering directly from the book text itself. Inquire allows the user to not only read and browse the textbook, but also to ask questions and get reasoned or retrieved answers back, explore the material through semantic connections, and receive suggestions of useful questions to ask. In this talk I will describe the project, in particular the textual question-answering component and its use of natural language processing, paraphrasing, textual entailment, and its exploitation of the formal knowledge base. I will also discuss the interplay being developed between the hand-built knowledge and automatic text-extracted knowledge, how each offers complementary strengths, and how each can leverage the other. Finally I will discuss the value of this approach, and argue for the importance of creating a deeper understanding of textual material, and ultimately more knowledgeable machines.

Visual Search and Analysis in Textual and Non-textual Document Repositories-Approaches, Applications, and Research Challenges

Tobias Schreck

University of Konstanz,
Computer and Information Science,
Universitaetsstrasse 10, Box 78,
D-78457 Konstanz, Germany
Tobias.Schreck@uni-konstanz.de

Abstract. Information retrieval and analysis are key tasks in dealing with the information overload problem characteristic for today's networked digital environments. Advances in data acquisition, transmission and storage, and emergence of social media, lead to an abundance of textual and non-textual information items available to everyone at any time. Advances in visual-interactive data analysis can provide for effective visual interfaces for query formulation, navigation, and result exploration in complex information spaces. In this presentation, we will discuss selected approaches for visual analysis in large textual and non-textual document collections. First, recent techniques for visual analysis of readability, sentiment and opinion properties in large amounts of textual documents, including promising application possibilities, will be discussed. Then, we will focus on visual analysis support for information retrieval in non-textual documents, in particular multimedia and time-oriented research data. We argue that new visual-interactive approaches can provide for effective user access to large document corpora, including discovering of interesting relationships between data items, and understanding the space of similarity notions for a given document repository. We will conclude the presentation by discussing research opportunities at the intersection of visual data analysis, information retrieval, and evaluation.

Table of Contents

Evaluation Methodologies and Infrastructure

Posters

Analysis and Refinement
of Cross-Lingual Entity Linking

Taylor Cassidy[1], Heng Ji[1], Hongbo Deng[2], Jing Zheng[3], and Jiawei Han[2]

[1] Computer Science Department and Linguistics Department,
Queens College and Graduate Center, City University of New York, New York, NY, USA
{taylorcassidy64,hengji}@gmail.com
[2] Computer Science Department,
University of Illinois at Urbana-Champaign, Urbana-Champaign, IL, USA
{hbdeng,hanj}@illinois.edu
[3] SRI International, Menlo Park, CA, USA
zj@speech.sri.com

Abstract. In this paper we propose two novel approaches to enhance cross-lingual entity linking (CLEL). One is based on cross-lingual information networks, aligned based on monolingual information extraction, and the other uses topic modeling to ensure global consistency. We enhance a strong baseline system derived from a combination of state-of-the-art machine translation and monolingual entity linking to achieve 11.2% improvement in B-Cubed+ F-measure. Our system achieved highly competitive results in the NIST Text Analysis Conference (TAC) Knowledge Base Population (KBP2011) evaluation. We also provide detailed qualitative and quantitative analysis on the contributions of each approach and the remaining challenges.

1 Introduction

The main goal of the Knowledge Base Population (KBP) track at the Text Analysis Conference (TAC) is to gather information about an entity that is scattered among the documents in a large collection, and then use the extracted information to populate an existing English knowledge base (KB). Previous KBP tasks were limited to mono-lingual processing; however, for certain entities, a lot of information is only available in documents written in a foreign language. To address this issue KBP2011 [12] included a new cross-lingual entity linking (CLEL) task in which queries from both Chinese and English are clustered, and whether each cluster corresponds to a KB entry is determined. The English KB used for this task is a subset of Wikipedia. Each KB entry consists of the title, infobox, and full text of a Wikipedia article.

There are two conventional ways to extend mono-lingual entity linking systems to the cross-lingual setting: (1) Apply a Source Language (SL) mono-lingual entity linking (MLEL) system to link SL entity mentions to SL KB entries, and then link the SL KB entry to the corresponding Target Language (TL) KB entry; (2) Apply machine translation (MT) to translate the SL document into the TL, and then apply a TL MLEL system to link entity mentions in the translated document to TL KB entries. These pipelines essentially convert CLEL to MLEL. However, these approaches are limited by

T. Catarci et al. (Eds.): CLEF 2012, LNCS 7488, pp. 1–12, 2012.

their core components: approach (1) relies heavily on the existence of an SL KB whose size is comparable to the TL KB, as well as the existence of a reliable mapping between the two KB. Thus, this approach is not easily adaptable to low-density languages. Approach (2) relies on MT output, and as such it will suffer from translation errors, particularly those involving named entities (NE).

In order to both enhance the portability and reduce the cost of cross-lingual entity linking, we have developed a novel re-ranking approach which requires neither MT nor a source language KB. Our research hypothesis is that the query entity mentions ("queries" from here on) can be disambiguated based on their "collaborators" or "supporters"; namely, those entities which co-occur with, or are semantically related to the queries. For example, three different entities with the same name spelling "阿尔伯特/Albert" can be disambiguated by their respective affiliations with co-occurring entities: "比利时/Belgium", "国际奥委会/International Olympic Committee", and "美国科学院/National Academy of Sciences". We construct a large entity supporting matrix to jointly mine and disambiguate entities.

In our second enhancement we adapt the distributional [10] and "One Sense Per Discourse" [9] hypotheses to our task: we hypothesize that queries sharing topically-related contexts tend to link to the same KB entry, and we consider the KB entry denoted by a query to be its *sense*, while treating a set of documents discussing the same topic as a discourse. Topic modeling provides a natural and effective way to model the contextual profile of each query [15]. Identical or highly similar entity mentions in a single coherent latent topic tend to express the same sense, and thus should be linked to the same KB entry. For example, a query "*Li Na*" is associated with a sports topic cluster represented by, {*tennis, player, Russia, final, single, gain, half, male, ...*}, and an identical query, "*Li Na*", is associated with a politics topic cluster represented by {*Pakistan, relation, express, vice president, country, Prime minister, ...*}; thus, they probably refer to two different entities. We also observe that entities play a significant role in distinguishing topics. Based on these observations, our second CLEL enhancement employs a topic modeling method with a biased propagation (in which both entities and documents are assigned to topic clusters), to the Chinese source documents. In doing so, we implicitly assume consistency of results among entities in each topic cluster based on our second hypothesis: "one entity per topic cluster".

2   Related Work

Although CLEL is a new task in the KBP track, similar efforts have been published in recent papers [18], but with evaluation settings and query selection criteria that are quite different (precision and recall are calculated on a by-token, as opposed to a by-cluster basis; their queries are selected automatically by propagating NE output from English source documents to parallel documents in other languages via automatic word alignment, while KBP CLEL queries were manually selected to cover many ambiguous entities and name variants). Almost all CLEL systems participating in the KBP2011 track (e.g. [19,21,7]) followed the approaches outlined above (MLEL using a source language KB or MLEL on MT output).

Some previous work applied similarity metrics to or used links between each multilingual pair of names to summarize multi-lingual Wikipedias [8], find similar sentences [2], or extract bi-lingual terminology [6]. Some recent name pair mining work has been based on aligning Multi-lingual Wikipedia Pages [22], Infoboxes [17], and web co-occurrence based networks [23]. To the best of our knowledge, our re-ranking approach is the first work to apply unsupervised cross-lingual name pair mining to enhance entity linking. In addition, [20] used unambiguous concept mentions to bootstrap the linking of more ambiguous mentions based on Wikipedia link structure, but do not incorporate more fine-grained relationships between entities.

[15] applied topic modeling for the Web People Search task [1]. We extended this idea from the mono-lingual to the cross-lingual setting. The topic modeling method we use treats "entity mention" and "document" as node types in a heterogeneous network, where the topic distribution for a document is based on both its overall content as well as the topic distributions of the entity mentions it contains, which are completely derived from the topic distributions of the documents that contain them.

3   Task Definition

We are addressing the CLEL task of the NIST TAC KBP2011 evaluations [12]. Given a Chinese or English query that consists of a name string - which may refer to a person (PER), organization (ORG) or geo-political entity (GPE, a location with a government) - and a source document ID, a system is required to provide an English KB entry ID to which the name string refers. Queries for which no such KB entry exists are classified as NIL. Co-referring queries must be clustered (including those classified as NIL), and each cluster must be assigned a unique ID. KBP2011 used a modified B-Cubed metric (B-Cubed+) [12] to evaluate entity clusters.

4   System Overview

Figure 1 depicts the overall pipeline of our cross-lingual entity linking system. We have developed a baseline approach consisting of state-of-the-art name translation, machine translation, and mono-lingual entity linking. The baseline system first translates a Chinese query and its associated document into English, and then applies English MLEL to link the translated query, given the translated document as context, to the English KB.

We apply a Chinese name coreference resolution system [14] to each source document in order to get name variants for a given query. Then we apply various name translation approaches including name transliteration, name mining from comparable corpora and information extraction based name re-ranking, as described in [13].

We then apply a hierarchical phrase-based machine translation system as described in [24] to translate Chinese documents to English. The system is based on a weighted synchronous context-free grammar (SCFG). All SCFG rules are associated with a set of features that are used to compute derivation probabilities under a log-linear model. The scaling factors for all features are optimized by minimum error rate training (MERT) to maximize BLEU score. Given an input sentence in the source language, translation

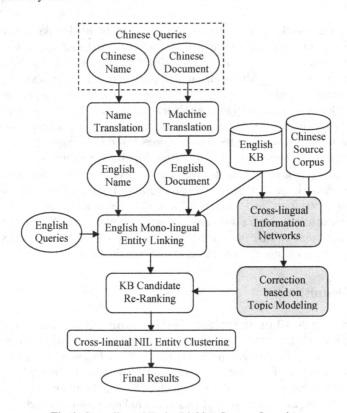

Fig. 1. Cross-lingual Entity Linking System Overview

into the target language is cast as a search problem, where the goal is to find the highest-probability derivation that generates the source-side sentence, using the rules in the SCFG. A CKY-style decoder was used to solve the search problem.

After translating the queries and documents into English, we apply a high-performing English MLEL system [4] to link each query. This system includes two unsupervised rankers based on entity profile and document similarity features, and three supervised rankers(Maximum Entropy, Support Vector Machines and ListNet) based on surface features, document features, and profiling features (entity attributes that are extracted by a slot filling system).

We then developed a novel joint approach for translating and disambiguating entities through cross-lingual information network construction (section 5). From the information networks we can extract a context similarity score for each query, KB entry pair. This context similarity score is then combined with the MLEL scores (i.e. the results of applying MLEL to MT output) based on weights optimized from the KBP2011 training data set. In addition, we applied a new entity-driven topic modeling approach with biased propagation [5], to ensure the consistency of entity linking results within each topic cluster (section 6).

Finally, we implemented a simple substring matching based approach to NIL clustering. For Chinese queries, we apply a within-document Chinese coreference resolution system and some abbreviation gazetteers to expand each query (e.g.

"魁北克/Quebec"), yielding a cluster of coreferential names ("魁北克, 魁北克集团/Quebec, Quebec group") for greedy matching.

5   Information Networks for CLEL

5.1   Motivations

As we pointed out in the introduction, both basic approaches to CLEL present problems. In addition, there are some characteristics specific to Chinese that can be addressed by adding more fine-grained contexts as ranking features. For example, when foreign politician names appear in Chinese documents, they normally only include last names. To some extent this introduces extra ambiguities to the cross-lingual setting.

Some entity mentions are more difficult to translate than others due to referential ambiguity. However, entity mentions can be disambiguated based on co-occurring entity mentions that are less ambiguous. When a human determines the referent of a query, one strategy is to first construct its *profile* from the text. This might include its title, origin, employer or social affiliations in the case of a person, or location and capital city in the case of a country, etc. To the extent that the corresponding relationships between queries and co-occurring entity mentions are significant, we expect them to be reflected in the KB structure (as relations between the target KB entry and other KB entries); thus, a query can be disambiguated by comparing a profile extracted from its surrounding text to profiles of candidate target KB entries, given in terms of the Wikipedia link structure, info boxes, and relations expressed in the KB entry's text. This method is reliable to the extent that the profile entity mentions are unambiguously associated with their own KB entries, and relations expressed in text are in fact expressed in the KB. If these conditions are met, unambiguous entity mentions can bootstrap disambiguation of more difficult cases in their profiles. Inspired by this intuition, we propose a novel approach to jointly mine entity translations and disambiguate entities based on entity profile comparison.

We exploit a representation called "Information Networks" [16] to model the profile for each query. This approach is effective for disambiguating queries with common organization names or person names to the extent that the query's profile is readily inferred from the context, and the profiles of competing target KB entries for a given query don't overlap. For example, if a query such as *"Supreme Court"*, *"LDP (Liberty and Democracy Party)"*, or *"Newcastle University"* has a country entity mention in its profile, it is fairly easy to disambiguate after comparing query profiles with candidate KB entry profiles. In practice, however, the extent to which entity profiles are explicitly presented varies. Table 1 presents the various types of contexts that may help disambiguate entities.

5.2   Information Networks Construction

For a given Chinese query, we refer to the other entity mentions in the associated source document that are associated with the query as its *neighbors*. Here, association can consist of either an automatically extracted relationship or simple co-occurrence

Table 1. Information Networks Examples for Entity Disambiguation

Context Types	Examples				
	Query	KB Node	Key Context	Context Sentence	Context Sentence Translation
Co-occurrence	塞维利亚 (Sevilla)	Sevilla, Spain	西班牙 (Spain)	西班牙两名飞行员 15 日举行婚礼，从而成为西班牙军队中首对结婚的同性情侣。婚礼在塞维利亚市政府举行。	Two pilots had their wedding in **Spain** on 15th, and so they became the first homosexual couple who got married in Spanish troops. The wedding was held in **Sevilla** city hall.
	民主进步党 (Democratic Progressive Party)	Democratic Progressive Party, Bosnia	波士尼亚 (Bosnia)	波士尼亚总理塔奇克的助理表示；... 在中央政府担任要职的两名他所属的民主进步党党员也将辞职。	The assistant of **Bosnia** Premier Taqik said ...two **Democratic Progressive Party** members who held important duties in the central government...
Part-whole Relation	Fairmont	Fairmont, West Virginia	WV	Verizon coverage in **WV** is good along the interstates and in the major cities like Charleston, Clarksburg, **Fairmont**, Morgantown, Huntington, and Parkersburg.	-
	曼彻斯特 (Manchester)	Manchester, New Hampshire	新罕布什尔州 (New Hampshire)	曼彻斯特(新罕布什尔州)	**Manchester (New Hampshire)**
Employer/ Title	米尔顿 (Milton)	NIL1	巴西(Brazil); 代表 (representative)	巴西政府高级代表米尔顿	**Milton**, the senior **representative** of **Brazil** government
		NIL2	厄瓜多尔皮钦查省 (Pichincha Province, Ecuador); 省长 (Governor)	厄瓜多尔皮钦查省省长米尔顿	**Milton**, the Governor of **Pichincha Province, Ecuador**
Start-Position Event	埃特尔 (Ertl)	NIL3	智利 (Chilean) 奥委会 (Olympic Committee) 选为 (elected) 主席 (chairman)	智利击剑联合会领导人埃特尔今晚被选为该国奥委会新任主席	The leader of **Chilean Fencing Federation** *Ertl* was **elected** as the new **chairman** of this country's **Olympic Committee** tonight.
Affiliation	国家医药局 (National Medicines Agency)	NIL4	保加利亚 (Bulgarian)	保加利亚国家医药局	**Bulgarian** *National Medicines Agency*
Located Relation	精细化工厂 (Fine Chemical Plant)	NIL6	芜湖市 (Wuhu City)	芜湖市精细化工厂	*Fine Chemical Plant* in **Wuhu City**

(note that co-occurrence is determined after coreference resolution). We apply a state-of-the-art bi-lingual (English and Chinese) IE system [11,3] to extract relations and events defined in the NIST Automatic Content Extraction Program (ACE 2005) program[1]. Each IE system includes tokenization/word segmentation, part-of-speech tagging, parsing, name tagging, nominal mention tagging, entity coreference resolution, time expression extraction and normalization, relation extraction, and event extraction. Names are identified and classified using a Hidden Markov Model. Nominals are identified using a Maximum Entropy (MaxEnt)-based chunker and then semantically classified using statistics from the ACE training corpora. Entity coreference resolution, relation extraction, and event extraction are also based on MaxEnt models, incorporating diverse lexical, syntactic, semantic, and ontological knowledge. In addition, we apply a state-of-the-art slot filling system [4] to identify KBP slot values

---

[1] http://www.itl.nist.gov/iad/mig/tests/ace/

for each person or organization entity that appears as a query in the source documents. This system includes a bottom-up pattern matching pipeline and a top-down question answering (QA) pipeline.

For a given KB entry, we determine its neighbors by first applying the above extraction techniques to the associated Wikipedia article, and then by utilizing Wikipedia article link information: any two KB entries are considered neighbors if a link to one KB entry appears in the text (Wikipedia page) of the other.

5.3   Information Networks Based Re-ranking

As alluded to above, a query's neighbors may refer to the neighbors of its referent in the KB. Therefore, low baseline scores may be boosted based on the high scores of neighbor pairs. In particular, when choosing between two KB referents for a given query, we want to give more weight to the KB entry whose KB neighbors are likely to be the intended referents of the context neighbors of the query in question. The baseline system generates N-Best KB entries for each query, with a confidence value for each hypothesis. For each link type (ACE relation, ACE event, KBP attribute or co-occurrence) in the information networks of a query and a candidate KB entry, we counted the number of matched context entity pairs, and used these statistics as additional features for re-ranking. Together with the baseline confidence values, these features are sent to a supervised re-ranker based on Maximum Entropy, which was trained using the KBP2011 training data.

6   Topic Modeling for CLEL

The information networks we constructed capture each query's local (within-document) context but fail to incorporate global (cross- document) context. A document in which an entity is mentioned will normally contain only a small subset of the information that could, in principle, be used to distinguish it from other entities. One way to alleviate this problem would be to simply construct links between entity mentions irrespective of document boundaries; however, this would likely do more harm than good due to noise introduced by ambiguous names. To capture entities' global context we apply an entity-driven topic modeling framework adapted from [5].

The underlying intuition, when applied to the task at hand, is that the topic of a document is based primarily on its own explicit content, but is influenced to some extent by the topic of each entity contained therein, each of which is determined based on the topic of each document in which it appears. To incorporate both the textual information and the relationships between documents and entities, we use a biased regularization framework in which regularization terms are added to the log-likelihood topic distribution, and are subject to the constraint that the probability of an entity having a given topic is equal to the mean of the probabilities that each of its containing documents have that topic. A regularization term for a given entity type represents the difference between the probability that a document has a given topic and the mean of the probabilities associated with each entity it contains having that topic. A loss function is defined as the difference between the topic probabilities for documents and those of the entities they contain, which is minimized via generalized expectation-maximization. Finally, each document and each entity is considered a member of the topic cluster whose topic it's most strongly associated with. As the regularization parameter approaches 0 the model is reduced to standard probabilistic latent semantic analysis.

For each source document we extract its metadata, as well as English and Chinese named entities, using a bi-lingual named entity extraction system [14] which consists of a Hidden Markov Model (HMM) tagger augmented with a set of post-processing rules. The number of topics was estimated based on the percentage of clusters per query in the training data. After extracting topic clusters, we applied majority voting among the queries which have the same name spelling and belong to the same topic cluster, to ensure that they each link to the same target KB entry. Thus, two queries with the same namestring can be linked to different KB entries only if they have different topics.

7 Experiments

7.1 Data

The Chinese source collection includes approximately one million news documents from Chinese Gigaword. The English reference Knowledge Base consists of 818,741 nodes derived from an October 2008 dump of English Wikipedia. We used the KBP 2011 Cross-lingual Entity Linking training data set to develop our systems, and then conducted a blind test on KBP2011 Cross-lingual Entity Linking evaluation data set. The detailed data statistics are summarized in Table 2.

Table 2. Data sets

Corpus		# Queries		
		Person	Organization	GPE
Training	English	168	253	243
	Chinese	649	407	441
Evaluation	English	183	269	303
	Chinese	641	441	399

7.2 Overall Performance

Performance on the cross-lingual entity linking task both before and after applying our enhancements are summarized in Table 3. Source language information networks and topic modeling have significantly improved the results for Chinese queries, especially for the person (PER) and geo-political (GPE) types. Performance on PER queries is significantly worse for Chinese than for English, mainly because the translation of PER names is the most challenging among the three entity types; however, our enhancements were particularly beneficial for this category in which our system acheived the highest score. On the other hand, we found that for some Chinese names, their Chinese mentions are actually less ambiguous than their English mentions because the mapping from Chinese character to pinyin is many-to-one. Therefore, Chinese documents can actually help link a cross-lingual cluster to the correct KB entry, which is the reason some small gains were achieved in the F-measure for English queries. The overall F-measure was improved from 65.4% to 76.6%.

Table 3. Cross-lingual Entity Linking Evaluation Results (%)

Entity Type	Chinese						English					
	Baseline			Enhanced			Baseline			Enhanced		
	P	R	F	P	R	F	P	R	F	P	R	F
PER	37.5	42.0	39.6	**65.1**	**73.1**	**68.9**	74.7	73.3	74.0	**76.3**	**76.1**	**76.2**
GPE	73.5	74.9	74.2	**83.3**	**83.9**	**83.6**	82.1	81.2	81.6	**82.1**	**82.3**	**82.2**
ORG	68.3	83.9	75.3	**69.7**	**85.7**	**76.8**	77.5	81.0	79.2	**80.3**	**84.9**	**82.5**
ALL	56.3	63.4	59.6	**71.0**	**79.8**	**75.1**	78.4	79.0	78.7	**79.9**	**81.7**	**80.8**

7.3 Discussion

In Table 4 we present the distribution of 1,481 Chinese queries in the KBP2011 CLEL evaluation corpus in terms of the various techniques needed to disambiguate them as well as their difficulty levels. The percentage numbers are approximate because some queries may rely on a combination of multiple strategies.

Table 4. Distribution of CLEL queries according to difficulty levels

	Type	Percentage		Type	Percentage
Easy Queries	NIL Singletons	7.6%	Linked by Enhanced Methods	Information Networks	62%
	Name Spelling	4.5%		Topic Modeling	5.9%
Linked by Baseline	Surface Context	12%	Remaining Challenges	Discourse Reasoning	1.4%
	Popularity-dominant Entities	1.1%		Background Knowledge	2.1%
	Entity Type	1.7%		No-clue entities	1.8%

– *(1) Easy Queries*

NIL singletons: About 7.6% of the queries are singleton entities (e.g. "中绿集团/Zhonglv Group", "丰华中文学校/Fenghua Chinese School"), in that they only appear in one query and do not have a corresponding KB entry.

Name spelling: 4.5% of the queries can be disambiguated because their full names appear in the source documents. For example, "莱赫.卡钦斯基/ Lech Aleksander Kaczynski" and "雅罗斯瓦夫.卡钦斯基/ Jaroslaw Aleksander Kaczynski","田中角荣/ Kakuei Tanaka" and "田中真纪子/ Makiko Tanaka" can be disambiguated based on their first names.

– *(2) Queries Linked by Baseline Methods*

Surface context: 12% of the queries can be disambiguated based on lexical features or string matching based name coreference resolution. For example, for a query "亚行/Asian Development Bank" that appears in the title of a document, a CLEL system simply needs to recognize its full name "亚州开发银行/Asian Development Bank" later in the document in order to link it to the correct KB entry.

Popularity-dominant entities: A few (only 1.1%) of the queries are popular entities, such as "路透社/ Reuters"; such queries can be correctly linked using popularity features alone.

Entity type: For 1.7% queries, entity type classification is crucial. For example, if we know "沙巴/Sabah" is a geo-political entity instead of a person in the source document, we can filter out many incorrect KB candidates.

– (3) Queries Linked by Enhanced Methods

Information networks: As we have discussed in Table 1, many entities (62% of the evaluation queries) can be linked based on contextual information networks. Such information is particularly effective for those entities that may be located in or affiliated with many different locations. For example, almost every city has a "交通广播电台/Traffic Radio", and every country has a "联邦法院/Federal Court", so it's important to identify the other context entities with which the query entities are associated. Information networks can be very helpful to disambiguate highly ambiguous geo-political names if we can identify higher-level context entities that subsume them. For example, there are many different KB candidates for the query with the common name, "海得拉巴/ Hyderabad"; we can correctly disambiguate the query if we know which place (e.g. " Andhra Pradesh") the query is part of.

Topic Modeling: Document-level contexts, including what can be induced from topic modeling, are important for disambiguating uncommon entities (e.g. when"哈姆斯/Harms" refers to "Rebecca Harms", as opposed to "Healing of Harms" which is more likely on a relative frequency basis). For example, for the following two entities with the same name"何伯/He Uncle" , which are in the in the same city "Hong Kong", we will need to discover that one query refers to "a man with surname He", while the other refers to "He Yingjie" based on their associated topic distributions.

Document 1: "其中,81岁姓何老翁昨趁假期,...何伯不慎失足跌倒.../Among them, **the 81 year old man with last name He**, ..., ..., **He Uncle** fell down..."

Document 2: "有位何伯,....此人是...创办人何英杰。/there is a person named **He Uncle**, ... This person is **He Yingjie**, who is the founder of ...".

– (4) Remaining Difficult Queries

Discourse reasoning: A few queries require cross-sentence shallow reasoning to resolve. For example, in a document including a query "三沙镇/Sansha Town", most sentences only mention explicit contexts about "三沙港/Sansha Port", and that it's located in "Fujian Province". These contexts must be combined, under the assumption that "Sansha Port" is likely to be located in "Sansha Town", in order to disambiguate the query,

Background knowledge: About 2% queries require background knowledge to translate and disambiguate. For example, if "梁泰龙"" refers to a Korean person then the

English translation is "Jonathan Leong", but if the name refers to a Chinese person the translation should be "Liang Tailong". Thus, the correct translation of a persons name may depend on his nationality, which might be revealed explicitly or implicitly in the source documents.

No-clue entities: Some challenging queries are not involved in any central topics of the source documents, and as a result systems tend not to link them to any KB entries; in addition, their mentions have no significant context in common. For example, some news reporters such as "张小平/Xiaoping Zhang", and some ancient people such as "包拯/Bao Zheng" were selected as queries.

8   Conclusions and Future Work

In this paper we described a high-performing cross-lingual entity linking system. This system made use of some novel approaches - aligning Chinese source and English KB based information networks and entity-driven topic modeling - to enhance a strong baseline pipeline previously used for this task. In the future, we will add more global evidence into information networks, such as temporal document distributions. We are also interested in incorporating additional source languages (e.g. the triangle links among English, Chinese and Japanese).

Acknowledgements The work was supported in part by the U.S. National Science Foundation grants IIS-0953149, IIS-1144111, IIS-0905215, CNS-0931975, the U.S. Army Research Laboratory under Cooperative Agreement No. W911NF-09-2-0053 (NS-CTA), the U.S. DARPA Broad Operational Language Translations program, the U.S. Air Force Office of Scientific Research MURI award FA9550-08-1-0265. The views and conclusions contained in this document are those of the authors and should not be interpreted as representing the official policies, either expressed or implied, of the U.S. Government. The U.S. Government is authorized to reproduce and distribute reprints for Government purposes notwithstanding any copyright notation here on.

References

1. Artiles, J., Borthwick, A., Gonzalo, J., Sekine, S., Amigo, E.E.: WePS-3 Evaluation Campaign: Overview of the Web People Search Clustering and Attribute Extraction Task. In: Proc. CLEF 2010 (2010)
2. Adafre, S.F., de Rijke, M.: Language-Independent Identification of Parallel Sentences Using Wikipedia. In: Proc. WWW 2011 (2011)
3. Chen, Z., Ji, H.: Language Specific Issue and Feature Exploration in Chinese Event Extraction. In: Proc. HLT-NAACL 2009 (2009)
4. Chen, Z., Ji, H.: Collaborative Ranking: A Case Study on Entity Linking. In: Proc. EMNLP 2011 (2011)
5. Deng, H., Han, J., Zhao, B., Yu, Y., Lin, C.X.: Probabilistic Topic Models with Biased Propagation on Heterogeneous Information Networks. In: Proc. KDD 2011 (2011)
6. Erdmann, M., Nakayama, K., Hara, T., Nishio, S.: Improving the Extraction of Bilingual Terminology from Wikipedia. ACM Transactions on Multimedia Computing Communications and Applications (2009)

7. Fahrni, A., Strube, M.: HITS' Cross-lingual Entity Linking System at TAC 2011: One Model for All Languages. In: Proc. TAC 2011 (2011)
8. Filatova, E.: Multilingual Wikipedia, Summarization, and Information Trustworthiness. In: Proc. SIGIR 2009 Workshop on Information Access in a Multilingual World (2009)
9. Gale, W.A., Church, K.W., Yarowsky, D.: One Sense Per Discourse. In: Proc. DARPA Speech and Natural Language Workshop (1992)
10. Harris, Z.: Distributional Structure. Word (1954)
11. Ji, H., Grishman, R.: Refining Event Extraction through Cross-Document Inference. In: Proc. of ACL 2008: HLT, pp. 254–262 (2008)
12. Ji, H., Grishman, R., Dang, H.T.: An Overview of the TAC 2011 Knowledge Base Population Track. In: Proc. Text Analytics Conference (TAC 2011) (2011)
13. Ji, H., Grishman, R., Freitag, D., Blume, M., Wang, J., Khadivi, S., Zens, R., Ney, H.: Name Translation for Distillation. In: Handbook of Natural Language Processing and Machine Translation: DARPA Global Autonomous Language Exploitation (2009)
14. Ji, H., Westbrook, D., Grishman, R.: Using Semantic Relations to Refine Coreference Decisions. In: Proc. EMNLP 2005 (2005)
15. Kozareva, Z., Ravi, S.: Unsupervised Name Ambiguity Resolution Using A Generative Model. In: Proc. EMNLP 2011 Workshop on Unsupervised Learning in NLP (2011)
16. Li, Q., Anzaroot, S., Lin, W.P., Li, X., Ji, H.: Joint Inference for Cross-document Information Extraction. In: Proc. CIKM 2011 (2011)
17. Lin, W.P., Snover, M., Ji, H.: Unsupervised Language-Independent Name Translation Mining from Wikipedia Infoboxes. In: Proc. EMNLP 2011 Workshop on Unsupervised Learning for NLP (2011)
18. McNamee, P., Mayfield, J., Lawrie, D., Oard, D.W., Doermann, D.: Cross-Language Entity Linking. In: Proc. IJCNLP 2011 (2011)
19. McNamee, P., Mayfield, J., Oard, D.W., Xu, T., Wu, K., Stoyanov, V., Doermann, D.: Cross-Language Entity Linking in Maryland during a Hurricane. In: Proc. TAC 2011 (2011)
20. Milne, D., Witten, I.H.: Learning to Link with Wikipedia. In: Proc. CIKM 2008 (2008)
21. Monahan, S., Lehmann, J., Nyberg, T., Plymale, J., Jung, A.: Cross-Lingual Cross-Document Coreference with Entity Linking. In: Proc. TAC 2011 (2011)
22. Richman, A.E., Schone, P.: Mining Wiki Resources for Multilingual Named Entity Recognition. In: Proc. ACL 2008 (2008)
23. You, G., Hwang, S., Song, Y., Jiang, L., Nie, Z.: Mining Name Translations from Entity Graph Mappings. In: Proc. EMNLP 2010 (2003)
24. Zheng, J., Ayan, N.F., Wang, W., Burkett, D.: Using Syntax in Large-scale Audio Document Translation. In: Proc. Interspeech (2009)

Seven Years of INEX Interactive Retrieval Experiments – Lessons and Challenges

Ragnar Nordlie and Nils Pharo

Oslo and Akershus University College of Applied Sciences
Postboks 4 St. Olavs plass, N-0130 Oslo, Norway
{ragnar.nordlie,nils.pharo}@hioa.no

Abstract. This paper summarizes a major effort in interactive search investigation, the INEX i-track, a collective effort run over a seven-year period. We present the experimental conditions, report some of the findings of the participating groups, and examine the challenges posed by this kind of collective experimental effort.

Keywords: User studies, interactive information retrieval, information search behavior.

1   Introduction

The INEX interactive track was run as a subtrack of the Initiative for the Evaluation of XML retrieval (INEX) every year from 2004 to 2010. In this track participating groups have followed a standard procedure for collecting data of end users performing search tasks in an experimental setting. This has made it possible to collect quite large data sets of user-system interaction under controlled conditions.

The INEX experiments started in 2002, when a collection of journal articles from IEEE was licensed for XML element retrieval experiments [1] to provide "an infrastructure to evaluate the effectiveness of content-oriented XML retrieval systems" [2]. The general assumption is that XML elements can be treated as candidate items for retrieval, similar to full text documents, document parts and document passages. The INEX experiments were designed following the TREC model, with a test collection consisting of documents, topics/tasks (submitted by the participating groups), and relevance assessments provided by the participants, thus making it possible to compute the retrieval effectiveness of different matching algorithms. Since its beginning several tracks have been introduced to the initiative in order to explore topics such as relevance feedback, heterogeneous collections, natural queries, document mining, multimedia; and also a track devoted to studying interactive information retrieval of XML-coded data through user experiments.

In this paper we will discuss some of the lessons learnt throughout the seven years of interactive experiments. We start by presenting the experimental conditions of the interactive track (hereafter the i-track). Then we will explore some of the findings made during the years. In the third part we will discuss the possible levels

T. Catarci et al. (Eds.): CLEF 2012, LNCS 7488, pp. 13–23, 2012.

of interpretation for INEX i-track data and finally we will point out some of the challenges and problems we have experienced.

2   INEX i-Track Experimental Conditions

The design of the i-track experiments has followed rather similar patterns throughout the years. The elements used are:

- A search system developed by the track organizers. Optionally participants in the track developed their own system for additional experiments
- A document corpus, often the same that was used as the test collection for the standard ad hoc-track
- A set of topics or simulated tasks to be searched for by the experiment subjects
- Questionnaires, either paper based or integrated in the online experimental setup
- A relevance assessment scale for relevance assignments by participants
- A system for recording transaction logs
- A standard procedure for data collection

We shall look at the details of each of these items.

2.1   The Search System

Since its beginning the i-track organizers have made available a search system for the participating groups to use. The system used in 2004 [3] was based on the HyREX retrieval engine [4]. The system was designed for XML retrieval and when queried returned a ranked list of XML components, where each component was accompanied with the title and author of the source document of the component, its retrieval value, and its XPath. In 2005 [5] the organizers switched to a system built within the Daffodil retrieval framework [6], which provided some improvements over the previous system, specifically with respect to handling of overlapping elements, improved element summaries, and supportive interface functionalities. The Daffodil system was also used in 2006 [7], but this year in two different versions; one using a passage retrieval backend and the other an element retrieval backend. In 2008 [8] and 2009 [9] the element retrieval version of Daffodil was also used. In 2010 [10] a new system was developed based on the ezDL framework[1], which resides on a server and is maintained by the University of Duisburg-Essen.

2.2   The Document Corpora

In total three different document collections have been used in the i-track. In 2004 and 2005 a collection of computer science journal articles published by IEEE was made

---

[1] http://www.ezdl.de/

available for the experiments. The same collections were used by the INEX ad hoc-track, with additional documents added in the 2005 collection (see Table 1).

In 2006 and 2008 the Wikipedia collection [11] was used, it consists of more than 650 000 articles collected from the English version of Wikipedia. The last two years (2009-2010) the Amazon/LibraryThing corpus was put together for the i-track: "[t]he collection contains metadata of 2 780 300 English-language books. The data has been crawled from the online bookstore of *Amazon* and the social cataloging web site *LibraryThing* in February/March 2009 by the University of Duisburg-Essen. The MySQL database containing the crawled data has size of about 190 GB. Cover images are available for over one million books (100 GB of the database). Several millions of customer reviews were crawled" [10]. This collection is currently also in use by the INEX book track.

Table 1. Document corpora used in the i-track

Year	Collection	Size (no of items)	Use
2004-2005	IEE journals	12107/16819	Ad hoc & i-track
2006-2008	Wikipedia articles	659 388	Ad hoc & i-track
2009-2010	Amazon/Librarything	2 780 300	i-track

2.3 Topics and Tasks

The topics or tasks used in the i-track experiments were developed for exploring a variety of research questions. Borlund's [12] simulated work task methodology was used to formulate the tasks in order to make it clearer for the searcher which type of context the task intended to represent. In Table 2 we see a summary of the task categories and the number of tasks to be performed by the searchers.

In 2004 a selection of content only (CO) topics from the ad hoc-track was selected. The topics were picked to represent two different categories of tasks, "background tasks" (B) and "comparison tasks" (C) [3]. The selection of categories was justified from studies that have shown that different types of tasks invoke different relevance criteria for assessing web pages [13]. It turned out that the 2004 categorization was not a "great success" therefore in 2005 task categories were simplified to "general" (G) and "challenging" (C) tasks [5] and tasks representing these categories were collected from the ad hoc-tasks. In addition, the searchers in the 2005 i-track were asked to formulate examples of their own information needs to be used as "own" tasks. In 2006, using the Wikipedia collection, the organizers wished to emphasize the effect of different task types and created "a multi-faceted set of twelve tasks [...] with three task types" [7]: "decision making", "fact finding", and "information gathering". These were, in turn, split into two structural kinds ("Hierarchical" and "Parallel"). The selection of task categories was based on work done by Elaine Toms and her colleagues [14]. In 2008 a new set of tasks were used, "intended to represent information needs believed to be typical for Wikipedia users" [8], the two categories were "fact-finding tasks" and "research tasks". With the Amazon/LibraryThing collection new task sets were introduced, in 2009 the searchers were asked to formulate a task on their own given the premises that they should find a textbook within a course they were attending. In addition two task categories were developed by organizers, "broad tasks" which "were designed to investigate thematic exploration" and "narrow tasks" representing "narrow topical queries" [9]. A similar design of tasks were used in 2010 [10], but the categories were now called "explorative" and "data gathering".

Table 2. Tasks used in the i-track

Year	Task categories	Tasks per category	Tasks per participant
2004	Background; Comparison	2	2
2005	General; Challenging; Own	3 (+ own)	3
2006	Decision making; Fact finding; Information gathering	4 (2 of each structure)	4
2008	Fact-finding; Research	3	2
2009	Broad; Narrow; Own	3 (+ own)	3
2010	Explorative; Data gathering; Own	3 (+ own)	3

2.4 Questionnaires

The questionnaires distributed in the i-track experiments have not changed a lot during the years. Experiment participants have been asked to answer the following types of questionnaires:

1. A pre-experiment questionnaire with questions about the participants' background, including demographic questions, education, search experience and experience with different types of information sources
2. Pre-task questionnaires with questions about the participants' task familiarity and the perceived difficulty of the task
3. Post-task questionnaires on the experienced task difficulty and perceived satisfaction as well as on system features related to the task
4. Post-experiment questionnaires on general system related issues

2.5 Relevance Assessments Scales

The recognition of relevance as a more subtle and dynamic feature in IR has led to the introduction of non-binary relevance assessments in IR system evaluation [15]. In the i-track experiments many different relevance scales have been used to try to learn about the relationship between elements, their context and how end users react to the levels of granularity explicated in XML retrieval systems.

In the 2004 i-tack experiments a two-dimensional relevance scale was used, it was designed to measure how "useful" and how "specific" the assessed element was in relation to the search task [3]. Each dimension had tree degrees of relevance which (with the additional value of "not relevant") made a total of 10 possible dimensions (see Table 3).

Table 3. The INEX 2004 i-track relevance scale

Value	Explanation
A	Very useful & Very specific
B	Very useful & Fairly specific
C	Very useful & Marginally specific
D	Fairly useful & Very specific
E	Fairly useful & Fairly specific
F	Fairly useful & Marginally specific
G	Marginally useful & Very specific
H	Marginally useful & Fairly specific
I	Marginally useful & Marginally specific
J	Contains no relevant information

In 2005, 2009 and 2010 organizers used a three level relevance scale, asking participants to state if the elements were "relevant", "partially relevant" and "not relevant". In 2006 and 2008 a two-dimensional scale was also used, although a bit different from the 2004-scale. This scale was based on the work of Pehcevski [16] and aimed to balance the need for information on the perceived granularity of retrieved elements and their degree of relevance, and is intended to be simple and easy to visualize [7]. Figure 1 shows how the system interface presented the relevance scale to the participants.

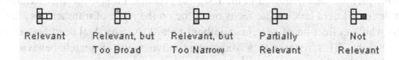

Fig. 1. INEX 2006 and 2008 interactive track relevance assessments scale

2.6   System Transaction Logs

For each of the experiments transaction logs have been recorded by the systems. These logs capture all events during seachers' system-interaction, including their use of search facilities, their queries, the query results, all elements viewed, and all relevance assessments made. The logs have been recorded as XML-files. In addition, some participating institutions have at different times used more sophisticated recording devices, such as screen capture programs to track mouse movements, or eye-tracking devices.

2.7   Data Collection Procedures

Data collection has followed a very similar procedure from each year to the next, the following procedure is quoted from [8]:

1. Experimenter briefed the searcher, and explained the format of the study. The searcher read and signed the Consent Form.
2. The experimenter logged the searchers into the experimental system. Tutorial of the system was given with a training task provided by the system. The experimenter handed out and explained the system features document.
3. Any questions were answered by the experimenter.
4. The control system administered the pre-experiment questionnaire.
5. Topic descriptions for the first task category was administered by the system, and a topic selected
6. Pre-task questionnaire was administered.
7. Task began by clicking the link to the search system. Maximum duration for a search was 15 minutes, at which point the system issued a "timeout" warning. Task ended by clicking the "Finish task" button.
8. Post-task questionnaire was administered.
9. Steps 5-8 were repeated for the second task.
10. Post-experiment questionnaire was administered

3   INEX i-Track Findings

Analysis of INEX i-track data has been reported in the annual INEX proceedings and in the SIGIR Forum, at conferences such as SIGIR [17] and IIIX [18] and in scientific journals, for example Information Processing & Management [19] and JASIST [20].

In principle, the data collected in the INEX experiments allow for interpretation on at least three different levels. The focus might be on the *types* of transactions / actions over the whole collection of searches, without regard to individual searchers or individual sessions. This represents a very quantitative view of search behavior, and includes investigations of how many times a text element on a certain level of granularity is viewed, judged relevant, with which degree of confidence, at what stage in the search etc.

Alternatively, the focus might be on *patterns* of transactions, again over the whole collection of searches. This approach attempts to answer questions such as what sequences of document or text element views precedes a relevance decision, how queries are developed and what influence factors such as the documents viewed in the search process has on query development, or where in the session a certain behavioral pattern occurs.

The third level of investigation would look at individual *sessions*, or sequences of interactions within sessions, to try to understand how factors such as user characteristics or types of search purpose influence actions, transaction patterns, or relevance decisions. On this level, quantification would be subordinate to a more qualitatively based analysis.

The research based on i-track data has in particular, not very surprisingly, focused on the element types users prefer to see when interacting with XML retrieval systems [17–23]. For the most part, this research has been based on the *type of transaction* perspective described above, and has examined the total corpus of search sessions as a set of countable instances of element views and associated relevance decisions. At times, these transaction counts have been subdivided by factors such as the task type or the systems' presentation format, but the perspective has still been to isolate the single transaction occurrences and quantify results.

Data from the 2004 i-track is analyzed in [21], the authors found that section elements were judged to be the most relevant element both with respect to specificity and to usefulness. In cases when both full articles and sections of the same article were assessed the articles were often assessed as more relevant that their section elements.

2005 i-track data are analyzed in [17, 19], which report that most users first accessed the "front matter" element (mainly containing metadata) when examining a document, but it is speculated that this should be interpreted as users wishing to obtain the full article first. In [23] the influence of topic knowledge, task type and user motivation on users element type preferences is analyzed. The authors find that users' topic familiarity is an important factor in estimating the type of task s/he is performing. [22] compared i-track 2004 and 2005 data with respect to how two different interfaces for presentation of query results (unstructured and hierarchically structured) impacts element assessments. The authors found that there was a stronger tendency for searchers to assess section elements, compared to other elements, when elements from the same document were scattered in the result list instead of presented structurally under the full article. [18] performed an analysis of interaction with the 2005 i-track Lonely planet collection, and found that that the major part of "exact" relevance assessments were made on elements at a more fine-grained level of granularity than the full document.

2006 i-track data was analyzed in [20], where it was found that larger units of text such as full articles and sub-sections were considered of most use for the searchers. The tendency was stronger for searches involving information-gathering tasks.

4   INEX i-Track as Model for Interaction Studies

There are obvious advantages to attempting the kind of collective, decentralized, semi-controlled experiment which the INEX interactive effort represents. It is possible, at least in theory, to collect a number of search sessions for analysis which would be extremely time-consuming for each institution to acquire on its own, and which, again in theory, should make it possible to draw quantifiable, not only qualitative conclusions. The data should be possible to compare across years, and be available for analysis by other than the initial experimenters. The relatively rich background data on the participating searchers should allow for quite detailed interpretation of the data.

On the other hand the decentralized data collection makes a controlled selection of searchers impossible, so that the sample will be self-selected. Even if the main research objectives are shared by the participants, the pooling of data also makes it difficult to have firmly stated research questions and thus establish and maintain the necessary control of the variables influencing the search activities under study. The research based on the INEX data has revealed a number of problems and challenges which need to be addressed in future interaction studies of this kind.

4.1   Tasks, Data and Systems

The *tasks* assigned to the searchers have attempted to emulate search situations which might conceivably call for different search behaviors and search result contents. The variation in tasks over the years shows the difficulty of finding a good theoretical fundament to base these distinctions on. It also makes it difficult to compare results across years. The challenge has been to find tasks that at the same time match real-life search situations, are uniformly understandable without specialist knowledge, are not prone to too much individual interpretation, and are sufficiently challenging to engage the searchers on whom the tasks are imposed. When searchers are given a selection of tasks intended to represent the same search situation, it is particularly important that these conditions are satisfied. In actual fact, even if searchers have been asked about level of task familiarity it has been difficult to control for differences in interpretation and level of involvement. In the years when a self-selected task has been included, it has been particularly difficult to specify this in a way which allows meaningful interpretation and comparison.

The choice of *database* has attempted to represent a set of data that is at the same time realistic and controllable and provides interpretable results. Again, the difference between the three data sets used makes comparison between years difficult. Relevance judgment is a very different task when applied to articles or parts of articles in a heavily technical domain as represented by the IEEE corpus, as opposed to relatively brief, well-structured and popularized Wikipedia articles, and judging relevance when the full text is available is again a different task from judging the relevance of books when only metadata are available, no matter how extensively the metadata represent them.

The concept of *relevance* in itself constitutes a challenge. The large variation in measures of relevance applied in the i-track over the years illustrates the difficulty of establishing a metric which is both understandable and applicable by the searchers, and at the same time measures with sufficient precision the success or failure of the behaviors or the system features under investigation. Since the main purpose of INEX has been to investigate the effects of the facility to present elements of text of different granularity to searchers, it has been important to measure some kind of degree of relevance related to the level of granularity presented. At the same time there is evidence that searchers are not able to interpret and apply a complex relevance measure consistently, and it is also difficult to determine which of the features of the complex measure to take into consideration when analyzing the interactions.

The *search system* has also varied over the course of the experiments. For the most part, searchers have been exposed to a system which they have not had the opportunity to use previously. This has the advantage of eliminating possible effects of system familiarity, but under the time constraints posed by the laboratory conditions of the experiments, it has been difficult to ensure a common understanding of system functionalities in the training time available, and the decentralized data collection further complicates a common presentation of the system or, in some years, systems. It has proven difficult to identify and isolate the effect of different mastery of the system as distinct from different search styles or different understanding of the tasks.

4.2   Units and Levels of Analysis

The abovementioned problem illustrates a major challenge with interaction studies in general and particularly with the i-track experiments: how is it possible to identify and isolate the features (of users, interfaces, tasks…) which may influence or explain behavior? Is it task variations, different understandings of the interface, different level of training, different level of interest in the experiment, differences in search experience, age or education, or other factors, which prompts certain actions to be taken or features to be used? To a certain extent, the responses to the questionnaires may clarify this, but the complex interrelationship between the factors is difficult to capture. This becomes particularly problematic when much of the interpretation of the data, as mentioned earlier, is based on counts of transactions or actions rather than on analysis of sessions.

A major challenge with the interpretation of the i-track data is the identification and specification of what constitutes a unit of analysis. In the logs, it is possible to identify individual actions, such as browsing a list of references, choice of an article or a smaller unit of text to view, etc. It is also possible to see elapsed time between actions. It is of course also possible to interpret these actions as parts of a sequence constituting a transaction, such as the series of browse and view actions which precede a relevance judgment. The difficulty is both to decide what sequences of actions should be considered part of a meaningful transaction and which are random sequences, how to delimit and define the transactions and how to agree on what constitutes a meaningful transaction. Also, there are actions that are important for understanding search behavior and which are impossible or difficult to determine on the basis of search logs, such as reading behavior, disruptions etc. Techniques for capturing such data have been attempted within the i-track framework, such as eye tracking, screen capture, thin-aloud protocols etc, but such data are not easily shareable, and they open new interpretational challenges of their own.

It has proven difficult to use the i-track studies to determine the usefulness of XML coding of text to support users' search. This is both because of the difficulty of interpreting the data with any degree of certainty, as discussed above, and because the concept of XML search itself is poorly defined – it is for instance difficult to distinguish a system based on XML coding from a passage retrieval system from a user point of view, at least as long as semantic XML coding is still difficult to attain and exploit. With all these constraints and their problematic features, however, the i-track data still constitute a rich source of interaction data which still only has been tapped to a certain extent. More importantly, the i-track data and the i-track experience might conceivably form the basis of the development of a framework or frameworks for user search investigation which may supply more firmly described and shareable data than those we have discussed here

References

1. Gövert, N., Kazai, G.: Overview of the Initiative for the Evaluation of XML retrieval (INEX) 2002. Presented at the INEX Workshop (2002)
2. Kazai, G., Lalmas, M., Fuhr, N., Gövert, N.: A report on the first year of the INitiative for the evaluation of XML retrieval (INEX 2002). Journal of the American Society for Information Science and Technology 55, 551–556 (2004)
3. Tombros, A., Larsen, B., Malik, S.: The Interactive Track at INEX 2004. In: Fuhr, N., Lalmas, M., Malik, S., Szlávik, Z. (eds.) INEX 2004. LNCS, vol. 3493, pp. 410–423. Springer, Heidelberg (2005)
4. Fuhr, N., Gövert, N., Großjohann, K.: HyREX: Hyper-media Retrieval Engine for XML. University of Dortmund, Computer Science (2002)
5. Larsen, B., Malik, S., Tombros, A.: The Interactive Track at INEX 2005. In: Fuhr, N., Lalmas, M., Malik, S., Kazai, G. (eds.) INEX 2005. LNCS, vol. 3977, pp. 398–410. Springer, Heidelberg (2006)
6. Gövert, N., Fuhr, N., Klas, C.-P.: Daffodil: Distributed Agents for User-Friendly Access of Digital Libraries. In: Borbinha, J.L., Baker, T. (eds.) ECDL 2000. LNCS, vol. 1923, pp. 352–355. Springer, Heidelberg (2000)
7. Malik, S., Tombros, A., Larsen, B.: The Interactive Track at INEX 2006. In: Fuhr, N., Lalmas, M., Trotman, A. (eds.) INEX 2006. LNCS, vol. 4518, pp. 387–399. Springer, Heidelberg (2007)
8. Pharo, N., Nordlie, R., Fachry, K.N.: Overview of the INEX 2008 Interactive Track. In: Geva, S., Kamps, J., Trotman, A. (eds.) INEX 2008. LNCS, vol. 5631, pp. 300–313. Springer, Heidelberg (2009)
9. Pharo, N., Nordlie, R., Fuhr, N., Beckers, T., Fachry, K.N.: Overview of the INEX 2009 Interactive Track. In: Geva, S., Kamps, J., Trotman, A. (eds.) INEX 2009. LNCS, vol. 6203, pp. 303–311. Springer, Heidelberg (2010)
10. Pharo, N., Beckers, T., Nordlie, R., Fuhr, N.: Overview of the INEX 2010 Interactive Track. In: Geva, S., Kamps, J., Schenkel, R., Trotman, A. (eds.) INEX 2010. LNCS, vol. 6932, pp. 227–235. Springer, Heidelberg (2011)
11. Denoyer, L., Gallinari, P.: The Wikipedia XML corpus. SIGIR Forum 40, 64–69 (2006)
12. Borlund, P.: Evaluation of interactive information retrieval systems. Abo Akademis Forlag (2000)
13. Tombros, A., Ruthven, I., Jose, J.M.: How users assess Web pages for information seeking. Journal of the American Society for Information Science and Technology 56, 327–344 (2005)
14. Toms, E.G., O'Brien, H., Mackenzie, T., Jordan, C., Freund, L., Toze, S., Dawe, E., MacNutt, A.: Task Effects on Interactive Search: The Query Factor. In: Fuhr, N., Kamps, J., Lalmas, M., Trotman, A. (eds.) INEX 2007. LNCS, vol. 4862, pp. 359–372. Springer, Heidelberg (2008)

15. Järvelin, K., Kekäläinen, J.: IR evaluation methods for retrieving highly relevant documents. In: Proceedings of the 23rd Annual International ACM SIGIR Conference on Research and Development in Information Retrieval, SIGIR 2000, Athens, Greece, pp. 41–48 (2000)
16. Pehcevski, J.: Relevance in XML Retrieval: The User Perspective. In: Trotman, A., Geva, S. (eds.) Proceedings of the SIGIR 2006 Workshop on XML Element Retrieval Methodology. University of Otago, Dunedin (2006)
17. Larsen, B., Tombros, A., Malik, S.: Is XML retrieval meaningful to users?: searcher preferences for full documents vs. elements. In: Proceedings of the 29th Annual International ACM SIGIR Conference on Research and Development in Information Retrieval, pp. 663–664. ACM, New York (2006)
18. Hammer-Aebi, B., Christensen, K.W., Lund, H., Larsen, B.: Users, structured documents and overlap: interactive searching of elements and the influence of context on search behaviour. In: Proceedings of the 1st International Conference on Information Interaction in Context, pp. 46–55. ACM, New York (2006)
19. Pharo, N.: The effect of granularity and order in XML element retrieval. Information Processing and Management 44, 1732–1740 (2008)
20. Pharo, N., Krahn, A.: The effect of task type on preferred element types in an XML-based retrieval system. Journal of the American Society for Information Science and Technology 62, 1717–1726 (2011)
21. Pharo, N., Nordlie, R.: Context Matters: An Analysis of Assessments of XML Documents. In: Crestani, F., Ruthven, I. (eds.) CoLIS 2005. LNCS, vol. 3507, pp. 238–248. Springer, Heidelberg (2005)
22. Kim, H., Son, H.: Users Interaction with the Hierarchically Structured Presentation in XML Document Retrieval. In: Fuhr, N., Lalmas, M., Malik, S., Kazai, G. (eds.) INEX 2005. LNCS, vol. 3977, pp. 422–431. Springer, Heidelberg (2006)
23. Ramírez, G., de Vries, A.P.: Relevant contextual features in XML retrieval. In: Proceedings of the 1st International Conference on Information Interaction in Context, pp. 56–65. ACM, New York (2006)

Bringing the Algorithms to the Data: Cloud–Based Benchmarking for Medical Image Analysis

Allan Hanbury[1], Henning Müller[2], Georg Langs[3], Marc André Weber[4], Bjoern H. Menze[5], and Tomas Salas Fernandez[6]

[1] Vienna University of Technology, Austria
[2] University of Applied Sciences Western Switzerland (HES–SO), Switzerland
[3] CIR, Dep. of Radiology, Medical University of Vienna, Austria
[4] Radiology Department, University of Heidelberg, Germany
[5] ETHZ, Zürich, Switzerland
[6] Gencat, Spain
henning.mueller@hevs.ch

Abstract. Benchmarks have shown to be an important tool to advance science in the fields of information analysis and retrieval. Problems of running benchmarks include obtaining large amounts of data, annotating it and then distributing it to the participants of a benchmark. Distribution of the data to participants is currently mostly done via data download that can take hours for large data sets and in countries with slow Internet connections even days. Sending physical hard disks was also used for distributing very large scale data sets (for example by TRECvid) but also this becomes infeasible if the data sets reach sizes of 5–10 TB. With cloud computing it is possible to make very large data sets available in a central place with limited costs. Instead of distributing the data to the participants, the participants can compute their algorithms on virtual machines of the cloud providers. This text presents reflections and ideas of a concrete project on using cloud–based benchmarking paradigms for medical image analysis and retrieval. It is planned to run two evaluation campaigns in 2013 and 2014 using the proposed technology.

Keywords: benchmark, medical image analysis, anatomy detection, case–based medical information retrieval, cloud computing.

1 Introduction

In many scientific domains benchmarks have shown to improve progress, from text retrieval (TREC, Text Retrieval Conference [4]), to video retrieval (TRECvid, TREC video task [7]), image retrieval (ImageCLEF, image retrieval track of the Cross Language Evaluation Forum, CLEF [5]) and object recognition (PASCAL [3]). Medical applications have also been subject to benchmarks such as ImageCLEFmed on visual data, to text retrieval from patient records in TREC. Impact of the benchmarks was shown in [6,8,9], both economically and scholarly.

T. Catarci et al. (Eds.): CLEF 2012, LNCS 7488, pp. 24–29, 2012.
© Springer-Verlag Berlin Heidelberg 2012

Data, particularly visual data, has been difficult to obtain for many years and thus data sets used for evaluation have often been small as a result. With the creation of social data sharing sites such as YouTube[1] and FlickR[2], obtaining large data sets has become much easier as many images are made accessible with clear licenses for their use, most often using Creative Commons licenses. In the medical field the funding agencies also push for open data accessibility and this means that data have now become available on a larger scale. Getting terabytes of data is in principle no longer a major difficulty.

The problem has rather become the annotation or ground truthing of large amounts of existing data that is often very expensive. In the case of medical data the ground truthing most often needs to be performed by experts, leading to even higher costs. Expert judgements are also a limitation for crowd sourcing approaches [1] that can otherwise help limiting costs for relevance judgements.

This text proposes solutions for the data distribution challenge by using an infrastructure based on cloud computing [2]. Bringing the algorithms to the data may allow for a better comparability of approaches, and it may make it better possible to work on sometimes restricted data. Virtual machines in the cloud that have access to the data allow all participants to use their choice of operating system and environment. Making code work in a different run time environment can sometimes be a tedious task and it can also limit participation. Having a similar virtual machine for each participant also creates the same conditions for all participants in terms of processing speed and optimization. In many standard benchmarks, the groups with a larger server capacity often have an easier task when trying to obtain very good results and test varying parameters.

Also the problem of ground truthing is tackled by the approach described in this paper, using a small gold (manually labelled) and then a large silver (fusion of participant submissions) ground truth set. Such a silver ground truth is planned to be generated through the results of the participants' runs in the cloud and can thus be created directly with the data and the algorithms. Putting such a ground truth together may lead to better analysis of techniques but there are also risks that the techniques of existing systems could bias the results in a similar way that pooling does.

This text also reflects on related ideas such as continuous evaluation when data remains available over a long term. Sharing environments might also help participants to collaborate and develop tools together and thus it can be a first step to facilitating component–based evaluation.

2 Materials and Methods

This article is mainly based on reflections of how to leverage visual medical image analysis and retrieval to a new scale of processing, starting with simpler tasks (such as anatomy detection) and very large amounts of medical data (on the order of 10 TB), and then moving toward more complex tasks such as the

---

[1] http://www.youtube.com/

[2] http://www.flickr.com/

retrieval of similar cases. All authors reflected on the topic to develop a new benchmark on medical visual data analysis and retrieval. The outcomes are based on all constraints of the system, such as very large scale processing and the requirement to generate ground truth with expert involvement. The results of this are planned to be implemented in an EU funded effort named VISCERAL[3] (VISual Concept Extraction challenge in RAdioLogy). This paper only includes reflections and only few experiences with the described methods. Experience from the first setup and evaluation sessions are planned to follow.

3 Results

This section describes the main ideas based on the reflections on requirements of a benchmark for such a large amount of data that require expert annotations.

3.1 Infrastructure Considerations

In terms of data distribution it is clear that going beyond several terabytes requires most research groups to change current infrastructures. Not only hard disks are required for this but also redundancy in case the disks fail, and quick access to the data to allow for processing in a reasonable amount of time. Cloud computing has the advantage that redundancy and backups are dealt with by the provider and not by the researchers. Access to the data can be given without the requirement to download the data and store them locally, so at any given time only part of the data is being treated making all data handling much easier for participants and organizers of such as challenge. The data can also be controlled better, meaning that confidential data can be used by the virtual machines and each use of the data can be logged, avoiding uncontrolled distribution. Participants can of course download small training data sets to optimize algorithms locally and then install the virtual machines for their specific setup, and run their algorithms on the cloud accessing the training data. This concept is also detailed in Figure 1. Execution will thus be in standard environments, allowing the evaluation of the efficiency of the tools, while groups with extremely large computing resources will not have major advantages.

The execution of the benchmark could then be done by the organizers by simply changing the path to the data in the tools of the participants and running the tools on the full data as shown in Figure 2. This has the advantage that 'cheating" or manual parameter tuning on the test data can be excluded as participants do not have access to the test data to use it for optimizations.

Such an infrastructure could also foster collaborations as systems can make services for specific tasks available easily and thus share components with other participants. This can help when some groups are specialized in text retrieval and others in visual image retrieval, for example. When the data can be made available long term, such an approach can also help creating a continuous evaluation where all groups using the data at later stages can submit their results via

---

[3] http://www.visceral.eu/

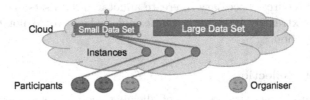

Fig. 1. The participants each have their own computing instance in the cloud, linked to a small dataset of the same structure as the large one. Software for carrying out the competition objectives is placed in the instances by the participants. The large data set is kept separate.

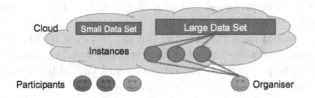

Fig. 2. On the competition deadline, the organiser takes over the instances containing the software written by the participants, upgrades their computing power, links them to the large data set, performs the calculations and evaluates the results.

a standard interface. The algorithms can then be compared for efficiency, and bias towards groups with much computing power can be avoided.

3.2   Silver and Gold Corpora

Manual work is necessary to create high quality annotation. In the medical field this is expensive but essential for good evaluation. By outsourcing the work to countries with lower income the costs can be reduced but quality control is necessary, as errors can lead to meaningless evaluation results. Sharing results among many research groups as is the case in a competition also leads to much more efficient annotation as data is not only used in a single center. All manual annotation cannot scale to millions of images and some automation in the ground truth generation will be necessary to allow for scaling.

Using the results of all participants directly in the cloud to create a so–called silver corpus in addition to a manually annotated gold corpus can make it possible to compare results based on two data sets and analyze how well the performance measures compare. The silver corpus can be created as a majority vote of the results of all participant runs directly in the cloud. One of the risks is that many systems using similar techniques will dominate the silver corpus. It can however also be an option that part of the silver corpus, for example documents with disagreement, can be manually judged to estimate the number of errors or inconsistencies in the silver corpus. Albeit not an optimal solution, such ground truth can potentially increase data set size used for an evaluation and limit the resources necessary to create annotated data sets. This can make evaluation on extremely large data sets feasible, which would not be the case without automation.

3.3 Further Reflections

Besides the purely technical reasons of allowing access to very large amounts of data there are several other aspects that could be improved by such a process. Research groups having less computing power are currently disadvantaged in evaluation campaigns. More complex visual features or data analysis can be extremely demanding in terms of computing power, so that many groups could simply not implement such complex approaches on large data. Measuring execution times has been proposed in the past but this is hard to control as the exact execution environment is rarely known. In terms of storage, currently few research groups would have the resources to process over 10 TB of data as not only the raw data but also computed data such as features need to be stored. Making available to participants the same types of virtual machines would give all groups the same starting point and full access to the data.

Another potential advantage of using a cloud–based approach is that public access can be limited to a training data set and then the virtual machines can be used to compute on potentially restricted data. This can for example be medical data, where anonymization can be hard to control as for free text but also intelligence or criminal data that cannot simply be distributed.

4 Discussion and Conclusions

When organizing benchmarks using extremely large data sets, using the cloud seems the only possibility, as the algorithms need to be brought to the data rather then the other way around. In terms of pricing, the data transfer is actually a fairly expensive part and renting computing power less so. Bandwidth is also a problem in many other environments such as hospital picture archives or data distribution to participants in a benchmark. Such a system allows for a better comparison of techniques and creates equal possibilities for groups from all countries, with fewer disadvantages if weaker computing servers are available for optimization. This can also avoid using the test data for parameter tuning.

Silver corpora can strengthen the effect that standard techniques and not new approaches will be used, a typical criticism of benchmarks. Still, academic research needs to start using extremely large data sets as problems on big data are different from problems on smaller amounts of data. For discovering these challenges big data and large corpora are a requirement. Contradictions and confirmations can be found by comparing the results with the gold test corpus and the silver corpus and analyzing what precisely these differences might mean.

The mentioned data volumes will allow moving closer toward using the volumes commonly produced in hospitals, which is in the order of several terabytes per year. Simple pretreatment is required to make algorithms scalable including parallelization techniques such as Hadoop/MapReduce, used in web search.

Still, most currently published research only uses very small data sets limiting the potential impact. Bringing the algorithms to the data and having research groups collaborate in the cloud on image analysis challenges will deliver new research results and has the potential to bring medical image analysis one big step closer to clinical routine.

Acknowledgments. This work was supported by the EU in the FP7 through the VISCERAL (318068), PROMISE (258191) and Khresmoi (257528) projects.

References

1. Alonso, O., Rose, D.E., Stewart, B.: Crowdsourcing for relevance evaluation. ACM SIGIR Forum 42(2), 9–15 (2008)
2. Buyya, R., Yeo, C.S., Venugopal, S.: Market–oriented cloud computing: Vision, hype, and reality for delivering it services as computing utilities. In: 10th IEEE International Conference on High Performance Computing and Communications, pp. 5–13. IEEE (2008)
3. Everingham, M., Zisserman, A., Williams, C.K.I., Van Gool, L., Allan, M., Bishop, C.M., Chapelle, O., Dalal, N., Deselaers, T., Dorkó, G., Duffner, S., Eichhorn, J., Farquhar, J.D.R., Fritz, M., Garcia, C., Griffiths, T., Jurie, F., Keysers, D., Koskela, M., Laaksonen, J., Larlus, D., Leibe, B., Meng, H., Ney, H., Schiele, B., Schmid, C., Seemann, E., Shawe-Taylor, J., Storkey, A.J., Szedmak, S., Triggs, B., Ulusoy, I., Viitaniemi, V., Zhang, J.: The 2005 PASCAL Visual Object Classes Challenge. In: Quiñonero-Candela, J., Dagan, I., Magnini, B., d'Alché-Buc, F. (eds.) MLCW 2005. LNCS (LNAI), vol. 3944, pp. 117–176. Springer, Heidelberg (2006)
4. Harman, D.: Overview of the first Text REtrieval Conference (TREC–1). In: Proceedings of the First Text REtrieval Conference (TREC–1), Washington DC, USA, pp. 1–20 (1992)
5. Müller, H., Clough, P., Deselaers, T., Caputo, B. (eds.): ImageCLEF – Experimental Evaluation in Visual Information Retrieval. The Springer International Series On Information Retrieval, vol. 32. Springer, Heidelberg (2010)
6. Rowe, B.R., Wood, D.W., Link, A.N., Simoni, D.A.: Economic impact assessment of NIST's Text REtrieval Conference (TREC) Program. Tech. Rep. Project Number 0211875, RTI International (2010)
7. Smeaton, A.F., Kraaij, W., Over, P.: TRECVID 2003: An overview. In: Proceedings of the TRECVID 2003 Conference (December 2003)
8. Thornley, C.V., Johnson, A.C., Smeaton, A.F., Lee, H.: The scholarly impact of TRECVid (2003–2009). JASIST 62(4), 613–627 (2011)
9. Tsikrika, T., Seco de Herrera, A.G., Müller, H.: Assessing the Scholarly Impact of ImageCLEF. In: Forner, P., Gonzalo, J., Kekäläinen, J., Lalmas, M., de Rijke, M. (eds.) CLEF 2011. LNCS, vol. 6941, pp. 95–106. Springer, Heidelberg (2011)

Going beyond CLEF-IP: The 'Reality' for Patent Searchers?

Julia J. Jürgens[1], Preben Hansen[2], and Christa Womser-Hacker[1]

[1] University of Hildesheim,
Department of Information Science and Natural Language Processing,
Marienburger Platz 22, DE-31141 Hildesheim
{juerge,womser}@uni-hildesheim.de
[2] Swedish Institute of Computer Science, Isafjordsgatan 22, SE-164 28 Kista
preben@sics.se

Abstract. This paper gives an overview of several different approaches that have been applied by participants in the CLEF-IP evaluation initiative. On this basis, it is suggested that other techniques and experimental paradigms could be helpful in further improving the results and making the experiments more realistic. The field of information seeking is therefore incorporated and its potential gain for patent retrieval explained. Furthermore, the different search tasks that are undertaken by patent searchers are introduced as possible use cases. They can serve as a basis for development in patent retrieval research in that they present the diverse scenarios with their special characteristics and give the research community therefore a realistic picture of the patent user's work.

1 Introduction

The retrieval of patent documents is a very complex and challenging task. Patent searchers are often expected to find (almost) all relevant documents in a very limited time frame. The sheer amount of already available patent documents makes ways of supporting the professionals indispensable.

Evaluation initiatives like CLEF[1] and NTCIR[2] have been trying to promote algorithms that facilitate the retrieval of patents. Many different approaches have been undertaken but during the three CLEF-IP periods there is no real breakthrough visible. Also, it is not completely clear how representative the data basis and the relevance assessments are so that it is difficult to estimate how realistic the results are. In the light of the so far applied approaches, which will be explained in section 2, it is reasonable to make further efforts in alternative strategies that can be utilized in patent retrieval and that may be useful in combination with existing methods. An idea for another approach could be the integration of knowledge about the search processes that take place during the different search scenarios. To date, only two CLEF-groups [1,4] have made use of

---

[1] http://www.clef-initiative.eu/

[2] http://research.nii.ac.jp/ntcir/index-en.html

T. Catarci et al. (Eds.): CLEF 2012, LNCS 7488, pp. 30–35, 2012.

this understanding and they both performed well. The research area behind this idea is information seeking (IS) which will shortly be presented in section 3. The potential of IS for patent retrieval has been acknowledged but researchers haven't established a general foundation. Therefore, this paper suggests establishing use cases on the basis of the different kinds of patent retrieval scenarios that take place in reality (section 4).

2 Previous Approaches within CLEF-IP

A lot of groups have participated in the CLEF-IP and NTCIR[3] tasks. In this paper, a focus is put on the CLEF-IP experiments of the last three years. The table lists the different approaches used in the prior art search task and the classification task, detailed information concerning the tasks can be found in [8]. Since we see a potential in including knowledge of the working processes of patent experts in the experiments, a brief introduction into information seeking is given in the next section.

3 Information Seeking

Information seeking is commonly understood as studying the processes performed by a human involved in searching for information through different information channels, such as paper-based, human, and those involving electronic IR systems. Information-intensive work tasks in professional settings, such as the patent domain, usually involve complex means of handling information. Therefore, the combination of information seeking behavior and the patent domain has been acknowledged by a range of researchers [5,6]. The problem here is that it is difficult to grasp knowledge about the information seeking behavior since patent examiners usually don't have the time nor the interest to publish their strategies and let researchers observe or interview them since the disclosure of a searcher's expertise and his strategies is often a delicate matter. This may be one of the reasons why no general foundation or model has been established for future research. This paper wants to contribute to filling these gaps by suggesting a model and presenting different use cases.

Information seeking models can be very helpful for understanding the different processes that take place in certain tasks. One of these models, developed by Marchionini (1995) [24], represents the search process in the patent domain quite well and could therefore be used as one possible model (see Fig. 1). Besides models, there is a need for knowledge about these processes to enhance our understanding of factors affecting information handling processes. For this reason, the different scenarios that patent searchers are confronted with have been analyzed. They will be presented in the next section.

---

[3] A brief overview of the NTCIR 4-6 techniques for the invalidity task are given in [7].

Table 1. Overview of the Approaches used in CLEF-IP 2009-2011

Type	Approach	Notes
Pre-processing	 – stemming – tokenization – removal of stopwords (language-specific, field-specific [9]) – removal of digits, non-content [10] – removal of punctuation, lowercasing [11], – use of n-grams [13] – compound and sentence splitting [14]	-
Linguistic approaches	 – extraction of keywords [1] – extraction of co-occurrence terms [10] – extraction of different kinds of phrases [15,16] – integration of concepts and use of terminological databases [1]	extraction of useful phrases remains a difficult task
Query and Document Representation	Fields used: – title, abstract, claims, description, classification data, inventor, applicant and applicants' countries [17] – structured index [9] – query length experiments [18,7,16] – patent summary using TextTiling [19]	experiments with different combinations of fields; 12% of the relevant documents don't share any words with the topic document [9], so word matching on its own will not be the ultimate solution
Use of Citations	use of citations in text [1,20,13,21]	legitimacy not clear, citation information generally leads to an increase of MAP but effects recall negatively [13]
Retrieval Models and Methods	 – frequency-based measures like tf-idf, RATF [4] – TextRank [21] – vector models [21] – regression models [1] – probabilistic approaches [22] – algorithms such as Okapi BM25, KL divergence [1] and COSINE [7]	-
Further Approaches	 – experiment with a passage retrieval system, that was originally developed for Question Answering [23] – integration of machine learning techniques to merge result sets and concepts coming from different sources [1,20]	interesting for this year's passage retrieval task
User-oriented Experiments	incorporation of knowledge about patent searchers [4], [1]	quite successful compared to other participants

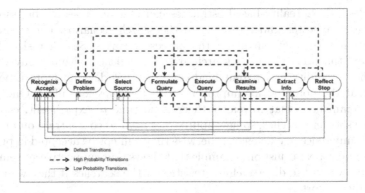

Fig. 1. Marchionini's model of sub-processes of information seeking (adapted from Marchionini 1995:50)

4 Search Tasks

The different search tasks have been described in [25,26]. Their explanations can be viewed as a good introduction but without the contact to real patent searchers, a few main questions always remain. In order to establish a more thorough understanding of the processes performed in patent retrieval, two former patent searchers were interviewed. They worked both in big industrial enterprises where they were active in different areas of expertise. Together, they have an experience of 32 years of patent retrieval and are both well versed in conducting all forms of searches. Since the general descriptions can be found in the literature, this paper focuses on the details discovered in the interviews. An overview of the characteristics of each search task is given below, they are listed in the following order: search task, institution that performs the task, point of time, type of documents used, scope, average size of result set, average number of relevant documents and average time needed:

- **Novelty/Patentability**: Patent offices, Patent attorneys, Research, Industry; Before patent application; Prior art; Worldwide; 500-1000; 2-3 can be enough for novelty, <50 for patentability; 1-2 day(s)
- **Clearance/Infringement**: Patent attorneys, Industry; Before market launch, then repeated regularly; Patents and published patent applications; Country specific or worldwide; a few thousand; 50-1000; 3-7 days
- **Validity/Opposition**: Patent attorneys, Industry; During a patent's life; Prior art; Worldwide; a few thousand; 50-1000; 3-7 days
- **State-of-the-Art**: Research, Industry; For strategic reasons; Prior art; Worldwide; a few hundred; 20-30; 1 day
- **Patent landscape**: Industry, (Research); For strategic reasons; Prior art; Worldwide; a few hundred or thousand; a few hundred or thousand; 1 week

These values are not to be taken as absolute values since some depend on the circumstances and can deviate. Hence they should be regarded as an orientation.

Nevertheless, these reality-based estimates can enhance research because they contribute to a better understanding of the search scenarios. For example, it is evident that the time spent on the processes varies. Search tasks like the novelty and the state-of-the-art search are often finished within a day whereas infringement, validity and patent landscape searches demand more time. This implies that the potential for improvement in the searches differs. One patent searcher commented that in reality there is no time to experiment, especially during the shorter searches, so new approaches need to concentrate on making a noticeable difference in efficiency, otherwise they will not be accepted in practice. The temporal aspect is just one example that shows that supportive systems need to keep an eye on the diverse characteristics of the searches if they want to be realistically supportive.

5   Future Research

It is obvious from the different use cases that there are a lot of starting points for future research. One possible way is to investigate patent search at real work places in order to understand patent searching from a more detailed perspective (e.g. [5]). This could also be valuable, since important aspects can be unfolded and highlighted. Further to the 'real-life' studies, one may develop models and frameworks, pointing out features to be investigated. Other focus points could be the different user groups and their requirements or the types and parts of documents used. Further research and knowledge about the work processes and the behavior of patent users should also be included in designing CLEF-IP tasks to make them more realistic. Knowledge on how patent examiners develop e.g. their information need, formulate their queries and make their relevance assessments, may guide the development of evaluation methodologies for patent IR.

References

1. Lopez, P., Romary, L.: PATATRAS: Retrieval Model Combination and Regression Models for Prior Art Search. In: Peters, C., et al., pp. 430–437 (2010)
2. Peters, C., Di Nunzio, G.M., Kurimo, M., Mandl, T., Mostefa, D., Peñas, A., Roda, G. (eds.): CLEF 2009. LNCS, vol. 6241. Springer, Heidelberg (2010)
3. Petras, V., Forner, P., Clough, P.D. (eds.): CLEF 2011 Labs and Workshop, Notebook Papers, Amsterdam, The Netherlands, September 19-22 (2011)
4. Järvelin, A., Järvelin, A., Hansen, P.: UTA and SICS at CLEF-IP. In: Peters, C., et al., pp. 460–467 (2010)
5. Hansen, P.: Task-based information Seeking and Retrieval in the Patent Domain. Processes and Relationships. Academic Dissertation, University of Tampere (2011)
6. Becks, D., Görtz, M., Womser-Hacker, C.: Understanding information seeking in the patent domain and its impact on the interface design of IR systems. In: Proceedings of the HCIR 2010, New Brunswick, NJ, August 22 (2010)
7. Graf, E., Azzopardi, L., van Rijsbergen, K.: Automatically Generating Queries for Prior Art Search. In: Peters, C., et al., pp. 480–490 (2010)

8. Piroi, F., Zenz, V.: Evaluating Information Retrieval in the Intellectual Property Domain: The CLEF IP Campaign. In: Lupu, M., Tait, J., Trippe, A., Mayer, K. (eds.) Current Challenges in Patent Information Retrieval. Springer, Heidelberg (2011)
9. Magdy, W., Leveling, J., Jones, G.J.F.: DCU @ CLEF-IP 2009: Exploring Standard IR Techniques on Patent Retrieval. In: Peters, C., et al., pp. 410–417 (2010)
10. Seo, H.-K., Han, K., Lee, J.: CLEF-IP 2011 Working Notes: Utilizing Prior Art Candidate Search Results for Refined IPC Classification. In: Petras, V., et al, eds. (2011)
11. D'hondt, E., Verberne, S.: CLEF-IP 2010: Prior Art Retrieval using the different sections in patent documents. In: Braschler, M., et al. (2010)
12. Braschler, M., Harman, D., Pianta, E. (eds.): CLEF 2010 LABs and Workshops, Notebook Papers, Padua, Italy, September 22-23 (2010)
13. Magdy, W., Jones, G.J.F.: Applying the KISS Principle for the CLEF- IP 2010 Prior Art Candidate Patent Search Task. In: Braschler, M., et al. (2010)
14. Szarvas, G., Herbert, B., Gurevych, I.: Prior Art Search using International Patent Classification Codes and All-Claims-Queries. In: Peters, C., et al. (eds.), pp. 452–459 (2010)
15. D'hondt, E., Verberne, S., Alink, W., Cornacchia, R.: Combining Document Representations for Prior-art Retrieval. In: Petras, V., et al. (2011)
16. Becks, D., Eibl, M., Jürgens, J., Kürsten, J., Wilhelm, T., Womser-Hacker, C.: Does Patent IR profit from Linguistics or Maximum Query Length? In: Petras, V., et al. (2011)
17. Teodoro, D., Gobeill, J., Pasche, E., Vishnyakova, D., Ruch, P., Lovis, C.: Automatic prior art searching and patent encoding at CLEF-IP 2010. In: Braschler, M., et al. (2010)
18. Toucedo, J.C., Losada, D.E.: University of Santiago de Compostela at CLEF-IP09. In: Peters, C., et al., pp. 418–425 (2010)
19. Mahdabi, P., Andersson, L., Hanbury, A., Crestani, F.: Report on the CLEF-IP 2011 Experiments: Exploring Patent Summarization. In: Petras, V., et al. (2011)
20. Lopez, P., Romary, L.: Experiments with citation mining and key-term extraction for Prior Art Search. In: Braschler, M., et al. (2010)
21. Verma, M., Varma, V.: Exploring Keyphrase Extraction and IPC Classification Vectors for Prior Art Search. In: Petras, V., et al. (2011)
22. Alink, W., Cornacchia, R., de Vries, A.P.: Searching CLEF-IP by Strategy. In: Peters, C., et al. (eds.), pp. 468–475 (2010)
23. Correa, S., Buscaldi, D., Rosso, P.: NLEL-MAAT at CLEF-IP. In: Peters, C., et al. (eds.), pp. 438–443 (2010)
24. Marchionini, G.: Information seeking in electronic environments. Cambridge Univ. Press, Cambridge (1995)
25. Adams, S.: Information Sources in Patents. KG Sauer, München (2006)
26. Hunt, D., Nguyen, L., Rodgers, M.: Patent Searching. Tools and techniques. John Wiley & Sons, Inc, Hoboken (2007)

MusiClef: Multimodal Music Tagging Task

Nicola Orio[1], Cynthia C.S. Liem[2], Geoffroy Peeters[3], and Markus Schedl[4]

[1] University of Padua, Italy
[2] Delft University of Technology, The Netherlands
[3] UMR STMS IRCAM-CNRS, Paris, France
[4] Johannes Kepler University, Linz, Austria
`musiclef@dei.unipd.it`

Abstract. MusiClef is a multimodal music benchmarking initiative that
will be running a MediaEval 2012 Brave New Task on Multimodal Music Tagging. This paper describes the setup of this task, showing how
it complements existing benchmarking initiatives and fosters less ex-
plored methodological directions in Music Information Retrieval. MusiClef deals with a concrete use case, encourages multimodal approaches
based on these, and strives for transparency of results as much as possible. Transparency is encouraged at several levels and stages, from the
feature extraction procedure up to the evaluation phase, in which a dedicated categorization of ground truth tags will be used to deepen the
understanding of the relation between the proposed approaches and experimental results.

1 Introduction

MusiClef is a benchmarking activity that will run as a Brave New Task in MediaEval 2012. Brave New Tasks are a new category of MediaEval tasks, meant to
pilot promising and new, but potentially risky tasks. After creating a test collection as a lab at CLEF 2011 [10], the collection will now be used for a multimodal
Music Information Retrieval (MIR) benchmarking activity in MusiClef 2012.

MusiClef is built around a *concrete real-world use case* centered around music
production. Stakeholders from this domain were involved in the original ground
truth labeling, and will remain involved at the evaluation phase.

Although copyright restrictions prevent original music audio to be shared,
MusiClef aims at allowing *replication of the results* by distributing both content features and the algorithms used to extract them. An initial set of features,
based on open source implementations of music processing techniques, is provided to participants. Additionally, it will be possible for participants to propose
alternative features that will then be computed on-demand.

Finally, MusiClef promotes *multimodal approaches* on the music objects. As
has been suggested before in the community [7], approaches going beyond audio
signal content may be necessary to properly address and solve real-world use
cases. Thus, besides audio features, related information in the form of social
tags and web pages will be provided, and participants are encouraged to include
other modalities and sources of additional information in their approaches.

T. Catarci et al. (Eds.): CLEF 2012, LNCS 7488, pp. 36–41, 2012.

2   Related Initiatives

The Music Information Retrieval Evaluation eXchange: The need for shared evaluation practices has been clear in the MIR community since 2004, when a first campaign on audio feature extraction was organized by Pompeu Fabra University at the ISMIR conference. From the year after, a very important evaluation campaign for this research was started by the University of Illinois: the Music Information Retrieval Evaluation eXchange (MIREX) [4]. Due to copyright restrictions, the organizers of the MIREX can only distribute publicly available test collections. For the rest, participants must locally experiment on their own test collections, after which they submit their software to be run on the evaluation set by the organizers. This approach has two drawbacks, which have already been debated by the MIR research community: the results of previous campaigns cannot be easily replicated and the performances depend on the individual training sets and not only on the submitted algorithms.

The Million Song Dataset Challenge: A recent relevant initiative to overcome music dataset sharing limitations is the Million Song Dataset (MSD). With the MSD, researchers can access a number of features from a very large song collection [3]. However, the feature set is fixed and the used feature extraction algorithms are not fully public, limiting possibilities to carry out further research on content description techniques. In 2012, the MSD launched a challenge[1] on music recommendation for which, similarly to MusiClef, multimodal and additional information sources may be used. However, despite similarities between MusiClef and the MSD challenge and the much larger corpus size of the MSD, MusiClef still validly offers a complementary alternative. With the professional use case from which the MusiClef corpus was built, manual labels attached to MusiClef items will be much cleaner than those of the MSD corpus, and more relevant to the dedicated practical use case. Furthermore, as indicated above, while not being able to publicly share audio data, MusiClef allows audio feature (re)computation on demand, allowing advancement on content description techniques too.

Quaero-Eval: Quaero is a program promoting research and industrial innovation on technologies for automatic analysis and classification of multimedia and multilingual documents gathering around 30 French and German public and private research organizations. Evaluation plays an important role in the program. In particular, Quaero-Eval focuses on audio and music processing, inspired by NIST and MIREX evaluations. Tasks to be run are defined upon common agreement, as are the annotated corpus to be used, the evaluation measures and the way the results will be published. A Mercurial repository allows participants to share and test the implementation of the evaluation framework and to access the training part of the annotated corpus. Submitted algorithms are run on the test sets using evaluation frameworks by an independent body that does not participate in the evaluation. Results are then communicated to the participants. After

---

[1] http://www.kaggle.com/c/msdchallenge

the evaluation has been run, the test sets are made public and an adjudication period starts in which participants can check in detail their results and comment on the annotations of the test sets. For each task, a report detailing the results is then written. A post-evaluation meeting allows participants to discuss in detail the results obtained during the campaign. The test set used for a given year becomes the training set of the following year. For comparison purposes, evaluation can also be performed on the test-sets of the previous years.

MediaEval MediaEval[2] is a relatively young, but rapidly growing benchmarking initiative that focuses on human and social aspects of multimedia. Originally established in 2008 as VideoCLEF, a track within CLEF focusing on the analysis of and access to multilingual multimedia content, it became an independent benchmarking initiative in 2010, adopting the name MediaEval and expanding the number of tasks. MediaEval strives to emphasize the *multi* in multimedia, including the use of speech, audio, tags, users, context as well as visual content. Because of this emphasis, MediaEval attracts a diverse group of researchers, both from industry and academia, with a large range of perspectives on multimedia research. MediaEval works by exploiting this diversity to drive innovation in task design and data collection development [5]. The main risk of MusiClef in the MediaEval context is that music currently is not commonly seen as multimedia data. However, we are strongly convinced that open challenges in music and multimedia research are very much alike [7], and thus intend to attract a multidisciplinary audience to the MusiClef benchmarking task.

3   Multimodal Music Tagging Task

Music auto-tagging is the process of automatically assigning semantic labels to music items (e.g., songs or artists). Such labels, or tags, can then be used for manifold music retrieval tasks, for instance, semantic text-based music search and faceted browsing of music collections, as well as for creating multimodal visualizations of music repositories. Typically, a machine learning approach, a *supervised learner*, is employed on a training data set to associate feature representations of music pieces with semantic tags. After training is finished, the classifier is used to predict labels to previously unseen music items. Most existing auto-tagging approaches for music take into account only one modality. Typically, content-based features extracted from the audio signal are used, for instance in [12,13]. Relying only on contextual, text-based features, a dictionary of music terms is used to index web pages and in turn assign tags to music artists in [11]. Mandel et al. [9] learn tag language models over different sets of vocabularies. With MusiClef, we aim at fostering multimodal approaches.

Task: The goal of the multimodal music tagging task is to exploit both *automatically extracted information about the content* and *user-generated data about the context* to carry out a tagging task: given the audio content of a song, a set of

---

[2] http://www.multimediaeval.org

social tags associated to that song, and a set of web pages associated to the artist that performed the song, participants have to highlight the tags that best describe the song. It is not mandatory, although encouraged, to use all the sources of information. The task is based on a real application scenario: songs of a commercial music library need to be categorized according to their possible usage in TV and radio broadcasts or web streaming (commercials, soundtracks, jingles). When this task is carried out manually, as it is still done by many companies, it is typical to exploit both audio content and contextual information.

Test Collection: The test collection consists of five parts:

−Songs: Because of the focus on multimodality, all the different sources of information should give a comparable contribution to the tagging task. Hence, one of the requirements for the test collection was to select well-known songs by popular artists. This way, we can expect that enough social tags are available for each song and enough web pages are available for each artist. We collected the songs starting from the "Rolling Stone 500 Greatest Songs of All Time", which lists songs that have been recorded by a total of 218 different artists. The initial list of 500 songs was increased by adding at most 8 songs for each artist, obtaining a final list of 1355 songs.[3]

−Audio features: For copyright reasons, content descriptors are made available through the distribution of audio features computed using the publicly available MIRtoolbox [6]. Participants may also request to use specialized features, and can submit their own feature extraction algorithms for this.

−User tags: The web service made available by last.fm has been used to automatically gather the user tags associated to each song. Tags are in the form of a simple list of terms.

−Web crawling: To offer another kind of contextual data, we performed web crawls using a major search engine to retrieve the URLs of the top-ranked pages for queries including artist and album names. Fetching the web pages corresponding to these URLs, we are able to provide music-related sets of web pages in different languages.

−Ground truth: Each song in the dataset has been manually annotated by music professionals, who routinely add textual descriptors to commercial music libraries. The vocabulary of tags was initially composed of 355 tags: 167 for genre and 288 for mood. Manual tagging was carried out through a web interface, from which it was possible to listen to the complete songs and select the associated tags through a number of checkboxes, divided in genre and mood. Annotators were required to provide at least one tag for genre and five tags for mood. From the initial set, we kept only the tags that have been assigned to at least 10 songs, obtaining a final list of 94 tags.

---

[3] For this campaign we purposely excluded live versions and covers, because the former can have a variable audio quality and the latter can give inconsistencies between tags related to the performer and web pages related to the composer.

4 Evaluation Procedures

4.1 Applying a Deeper Ground Truth Tag Categorization

It has been acknowledged that the types of tags that users add to music can fall into different categories, which do not relate to audio signal content in equal ways [1,2,9]. While a social tag describing a featured instrument ('guitar') can be inferred from the signal, this will be much harder for a personal tag ('seen live'). This is also seen in the ground truth tagging vocabulary of MusiClef. Tags like 'travel', 'club', and 'ballroom' have strong contextual non-audio connotations.

Other evaluation initiatives did not explicitly consider in depth yet the existence of multiple tag categories. MusiClef will do this, aiming to advance transparency and deeper insight into how different categories of tags may imply different feature choices and tagging approaches. Based on the final ground truth tag set, we propose a categorization more specific than 'genre' and 'mood' for MusiClef, partially inspired by musicological theories on film music functions [8], and touching upon different music aspects and potential use cases:

1. *situation*, time and space aspects of the music:
   (a) *physical situation*: concrete physical environments (e.g. 'city', 'night').
   (b) *occasion*: implications of time and space, typically connected to social events (e.g. 'holiday', 'glamour').
2. *sociocultural genre*, belonging to a certain *style*, with dedicated social communities identifying with them (e.g. 'new wave', 'r&b', 'punk').
3. *affective*, mood-related aspects:
   (a) *activity*: the amount of perceived music activity, without implying strong positive or negative affective qualities (e.g. 'fast', 'mellow', 'lazy').
   (b) *affective state*: affective qualities that can only be connected and attributed to living beings (e.g. 'aggressive', 'hopeful').
   (c) *atmosphere*: affective qualities that can be connected to environments (e.g. 'chaotic', 'intimate').
4. *sound qualities*, aspects that can clearly be connected to audio signal content:
   (a) *timbral aspects* (e.g. 'acoustic', 'bright').
   (b) *temporal aspects* (e.g. 'beat', 'groove').
5. *other*, for tags not in the above categories (e.g. 'catchy', 'evocative').

Tags may fall into multiple categories. A first categorization for the ground truth tags was made by the MusiClef organizers. This will be further revised after discussion with the task participants. At the evaluation phase, evaluation measures will not just be computed for the full ground truth set, but also explicitly be considered in relation to the proposed categorization above.

4.2 Reference Implementation

Participants can take advantage of a reference implementation that will be made available by the organizers. This implementation has two main goals: serving as a starting point for setting up a development code framework, and creating a baseline for participants to compare the effectiveness of their approaches. The reference implementation will be based on state-of-the-art auto-tagging approaches, without optimizations to maintain transparency.

4.3   Evaluation Measures

For a specific set of tags (possibly grouped into sub-categories), performances of the systems will be measured using both threshold-based measures (binary relevance) and affinity measures. For the binary relevance (tag-based classification), accuracy, positive/negative example accuracy, precision, recall and f-measure will be considered as measures. The affinity measure will be based on the Area Under ROC Curve.

Acknowledgments. The authors would like to thank David Rizo, of the University of Alicante, for his support in starting the MusiCLEF initiative. MusiClef has been partially supported by the PROMISE Network of Excellence, co-funded by EU-FP7 (grant no. 258191), by the Quaero Program funded by Oseo French agency and by the MIReS project funded by EU-FP7-ICT-2011.1.5-287711, and by the Austrian Science Funds (FWF): P22856-N23. The work of Cynthia Liem is supported in part by the Google European Doctoral Fellowship in Multimedia.

References

1. Aucouturier, J.-J.: Sounds Like Teen Spirit: Computational Insights into the Grounding of Everyday Musical Terms. In: Minett, J., Wang, W. (eds.) Language, Evolution and the Brain. Academia Sinica Press (2009)
2. Bertin-Mahieux, T., Eck, D., Mandel, M.: Automatic Tagging of Audio: The State-of-the-Art. In: Wang, W. (ed.) Machine Audition: Principles, Algorithms and Systems. IGI Publishing (2010)
3. Bertin-Mahieux, T., Ellis, D.P., Whitman, B., Lamere, P.: The Million Song Dataset. In: Proc. ISMIR (2011)
4. Downie, J.S., West, K., Ehmann, A.F., Vincent, E.: The 2005 Music Information Retrieval Evaluation Exchange: Preliminary Overview. In: Proc. ISMIR (2005)
5. Larson, M., Soleymani, M., Eskevich, M., Serdyukov, P., Ordelman, R., Jones, G.: The Community and the Crowd: Developing Large-scale Data Collections for Multimedia Benchmarking. IEEE MultiMedia (to appear, 2012)
6. Lartillot, O., Toiviainen, P.: A Matlab Toolbox for Musical Feature Extraction from Audio. In: Proc. DAFx (2007)
7. Liem, C.C.S., Müller, M., Eck, D., Tzanetakis, G., Hanjalic, A.: The Need for Music Information Retrieval with User-Centered and Multimodal Strategies. In: Proc. MIRUM (2011)
8. Lissa, Z.: Ästhetik der Filmmusik. Henschelverlag, Berlin (1965)
9. Mandel, M.I., Pascanu, R., Eck, D., Bengio, Y., Aiello, L.M., Schifanella, R., Menczer, F.: Contextual Tag Inference. ACM TOMCCAP 1(7S) (October 2008)
10. Orio, N., Rizo, D., Miotto, R., Montecchio, N., Schedl, M., Lartillot, O.: Musi-CLEF: A Benchmark Activity in Multimodal Music Information Retrieval. In: Proc. ISMIR (2011)
11. Schedl, M., Pohle, T.: Enlightening the Sun: A User Interface to Explore Music Artists via Multimedia Content. MTAP 49(1) (August 2010)
12. Seyerlehner, K., Schedl, M., Knees, P., Sonnleitner, R.: A Refined Block-Level Feature Set for Classification, Similarity and Tag Prediction. In: Extended Abstract to MIREX (2011)
13. Sordo, M.: Semantic Annotation of Music Collections: A Computational Approach. Ph.D. thesis, Universitat Pompeu Fabra, Barcelona, Spain (2012)

Generating Pseudo Test Collections
for Learning to Rank Scientific Articles

Richard Berendsen, Manos Tsagkias,
Maarten de Rijke, and Edgar Meij

ISLA, University of Amsterdam, Science Park 904,
1098 XH Amsterdam, The Netherlands
{r.w.berendsen,e.tsagkias,derijke,edgar.meij}@uva.nl

Abstract. Pseudo test collections are automatically generated to provide training material for learning to rank methods. We propose a method
for generating pseudo test collections in the domain of digital libraries,
where data is relatively sparse, but comes with rich annotations. Our
intuition is that documents are annotated to make them better findable
for certain information needs. We use these annotations and the associated documents as a source for pairs of queries and relevant documents.
We investigate how learning to rank performance varies when we use
different methods for sampling annotations, and show how our pseudo
test collection ranks systems compared to editorial topics with editorial
judgements. Our results demonstrate that it is possible to train a learning to rank algorithm on generated pseudo judgments. In some cases,
performance is on par with learning on manually obtained ground truth.

1 Introduction

Recent years have seen increasing interest in generating pseudo test collections
for training and evaluation purposes. This is primarily motivated by the costs
associated with obtaining manual relevance assessments. Most approaches to
generating ground truth leverage some kind of human behavior, such as annotation, hyperlinking, or simply using a search engine. Beitzel et al. [3] use the
Open Directory Project, a large scale annotation effort targeting web pages in
general. They assume relevance of documents to the title of the category they
are listed under to generate relevance judgments. More recently, Asadi et al. [1]
use anchor texts as queries and assume linked-to documents are potentially relevant documents. Web search is characterized by heterogeneous and high volume
content and usage data. We investigate the generation of pseudo test collections
in the less studied and more specialized domain of digital libraries.

Digital libraries are increasingly publishing their content online allowing people to access, browse, and search the archives. This type of content is typically
semi-structured and manually annotated using rich descriptors. These characteristics differentiate it from web documents, and many retrieval methods have been
developed to exploit them, improving retrieval effectiveness [6]. Modern Information Retrieval (IR) algorithms—especially in the form of learning to rank (LTR)

T. Catarci et al. (Eds.): CLEF 2012, LNCS 7488, pp. 42–53, 2012.

methods—are able to learn to combine relatively uncertain evidence from individual features and typically improve retrieval effectiveness when large amounts of training data are available [14].

In this paper, we focus on generating pseudo test collections which can be used to optimize retrieval algorithms for ad-hoc search on domain-specific, semi-structured documents. The most commonly used method for generating pseudo test collections is to sample and group documents in a collection by a certain criterion, and generate queries for these groups [1, 3]. In the domain of digital libraries, rich annotations are often available in the form of thesaurus terms, classification codes, or other descriptors that can be used as grouping criteria. Our leading intuition is that people provide this metadata in order to make documents better findable with regard to certain information needs. In this paper, we use such annotations to group documents in *topics*, and generate simulated queries (*pseudo-queries*) for and from these topics. The set of documents assigned to a topic is considered to be the relevant set of documents for the topic.

In the pseudo test collection generation process there are three key challenges that shape our research questions and contributions: (a) how to use annotations for grouping documents, (b) which documents to allow in the groups, and (c) how to simulate queries. The common, and cornerstone ingredient among these challenges is the sampling of annotations. Not all annotations are equally specific (compare, e.g., "United States of America" and "workaholism"). Developing methods for sampling descriptors from different metadata fields can help manipulating the generality and specificity of the resulting groups and therefore the resulting performance of LTR. In this work we tackle each of these challenges, using the domain-specific characteristics of ad-hoc search in scientific articles.

We discuss related work in Section 2. We present our methods in Section 4, conduct experiments in Section 5, report on our results in Section 6, discuss our findings in Section 7, and conclude in Section 8.

2 Related Work

We generate our pseudo test collections from the GIRT corpus. The GIRT corpus was first used in CLEF 2000 for the cross-lingual IR subtask [11], and later for monolingual domain-specific retrieval [12]. The usefulness of annotations as query expansion terms and reformulation was soon discovered [17]. Stemming and morphological analysis were the main emphasis in the CLEF 2007 monolingual version of the domain-specific task [5]. In CLEF 2008, groups using variants of pseudo relevance feedback managed to obtain the best performance [6, 16]. These findings suggest that the use of annotations can prove useful for simulating topics, and the adaptation of pseudo relevance feedback ideas can help in the query simulation process.

The issue of creating and using pseudo test collections is a longstanding and recurring theme in IR, see, e.g., [22, 23]. Over the years, several attempts have been made to either simulate human queries or to generate relevance judgments without the need of human assessors for a range of tasks. Azzopardi et al. [2]

Algorithm 1. Algorithm for creating pseudo test collections for semi-structured domain-specific collections

---
1: Sample an annotation dimension k.
2: Sample an annotation i from A_k.
3: Simulate query $q_{i,k}$.

---

simulate queries for known-item search and investigate several term weighting methods for query generation. Kim and Croft [10] generate a pseudo test collection for desktop search. Huurnink et al. [8] use click-through data to simulate relevance assessments, and later they evaluate the performance of query simulation methods in terms of system rankings [9]. They find that incorporating document structure in the query generation process results in more realistic query simulators.

In the realm of web search, Beitzel et al. [3] use documents listed under the categories in the Open Directory Project as relevant documents for queries that they generate from the titles of these categories. Most similar to our work is the work by Asadi et al. [1]. They use anchor texts to generate queries, and treat the documents linked to as pseudo-relevant documents for training a learning to rank system. Our work differs in the domain characteristics: we have no anchor texts, but we have rich metadata, like authors, co-authors, year of publication, keywords, and classifications.

3 Problem Statement

We first define the problem of generating pseudo test collections for semi-structured documents, and then describe our approach to this problem. A pseudo test collection is defined here as consisting of a set of generated queries Q and, for each query $q \in Q$, a set of documents assumed to be relevant, R_q. Given this definition, there are two main steps involved: (a) simulating the query and (b) simulating the relevant documents.

Our idea is to use the document annotations for this. Let a document d be annotated using k annotation "dimensions," each corresponding to a separate descriptor field. Each document has a set of $A_k := \{\alpha_{1,k}, \ldots, \alpha_{i,k}\}$ annotations corresponding to the k-th dimension. We can estimate a relevant set of documents $R_{i,k}$ for the i-th annotation in the k-th dimension from all documents that share $\alpha_{i,k}$. From the documents in $R_{i,k}$, we can also estimate a simulated query. This way of thinking about the problem breaks it down to the subproblems listed in Algorithm 1.

Our goal is to develop sampling methods that optimize the effectiveness of a learning to rank system in the setting of semi-structured domain-specific retrieval. In contrast to other pseudo test collection research, we are not primarily interested in developing methods that produce pseudo test collections similar to manually crafted test collections. We choose to evaluate our methods on the end-to-end performance of an LTR system, i.e., train on pseudo test collections generated by our methods, and test on manually crafted collections.

4   Sampling Methods

Below we discuss instantiations for all the steps in Algorithm 1; we begin with sampling an annotation dimension (STEP 1), then sampling annotations (STEP 2), and simulating queries (STEP 3).

STEP 1: Sampling annotation dimensions. We start with Step 1 in Algorithm 1. In the GIRT collection, there are three main annotation dimensions: METHOD can be any of 40 research methods, e.g., "descriptive study," CLASSIFICATION is a a classification code, e.g., "Labor Market Policy," and CONTROLLED is a thesaurus term, e.g., "social partnership." The first two (METHOD, CLASSIFICATION) dimensions cover broad topics, while annotations from CONTROLLED range from very broad to very narrow topics.

We sample annotations in two ways: from each dimension individually, and from all dimensions simultaneously. In the first case, we generate pseudo test collections using only annotations from one dimension, CONTROLLED, because it offers a range of more general and more specific coverage, just like we would expect in queries. In the second case, we take the cross product $A_{METHOD} \times A_{CLASSIFICATION} \times A_{CONTROLLED}$ and the relevant sets of documents consist of documents that are annotated with the triple of annotations over the three dimensions.

STEP 2: Sampling annotations. For Step 2 of Algorithm 1 we use two techniques for sampling annotations from annotation dimension CONTROLLED: randomly sampling single annotations, and randomly sampling pairs of annotations (sampling from $A_{CONTROLLED} \times A_{CONTROLLED}$), where the relevant sets of documents have both annotations. In the first case we observed that annotations ranged from broad to specific. Very specific annotations were associated with a very small number of documents, while some others were found very broad and were associated with a large fraction of the documents in the collection. Our second sampling method using pairs of annotations aims at accounting for this phenomenon: documents that have both annotations are intuitively more on topic than documents that have only one of the two.[1] Our third sampling strategy samples annotations from $A_{METHOD} \times A_{CLASSIFICATION} \times A_{CONTROLLED}$, as already noted above. In all three cases, to ensure that our sampled annotations are neither too broad or too specific, we select single annotations or pairs of annotations that are associated with between 100 and 1000 documents. The lower bound warrants enough training examples for the learning to rank system, while the upper bound discards very broad annotations.

STEP 3: Simulating queries. For simulating the queries in STEP 3 of Algorithm 1, we use two approaches: (i) use the annotations as queries, and (ii) extract query terms from the simulated relevant set of documents.

---

[1] We also experimented with sampling using larger numbers of annotations. The number of documents associated with them was found small, therefore of little use for training LTR systems.

Our first query simulation method is straightforward. Query terms are sampled from the content of sampled annotation(s). Our second simulation method is inspired by the observation that pseudo relevance feedback helps to improve retrieval effectiveness [6]. For extracting query terms from the relevant set of documents, we choose to use the log-likelihood ratio (LLR) score [15]. Our choice is motivated by the fact that most documents in the GIRT collection lack abstracts, which raises data sparsity issues due to the short length of titles. In this setting, probabilistic methods for query simulation [2] which build on language redundancy may prove less useful due to sparsity issues.

LLR is defined as the symmetric Kullback-Leibler divergence of the expected and observed term probability in two corpora, one being a background corpus. In other words, terms are ranked by how discriminative they are for both corpora. Stopwords, or common terms will rank lower because they also occur in the background corpus. For our purposes, we set one corpus to be documents in the relevant set $R_{i,k}$, and the other to consist of the rest of the documents in the collection. For every $R_{i,k}$ terms are ranked in descending order by their log-likelihood ratio score. To generate the query we take the top-T terms ranked by LLR. In all our experiments, T is set to 10.

5 Experimental Setup

We describe our research questions and the experiments we conduct to answer them. We evaluate our methods of constructing pseudo test collections with regard to their effectiveness for training an LTR system which is then tested on the GIRT collection *and* with regard to the system rankings they produce.

Our main research question is whether using annotations found in semi-structured scientific documents are useful for simulating relevant sets of documents, and queries for training a learning to rank system. We focus on the following questions:

Sampling methods. What is the effect of our sampling methods on LTR retrieval effectiveness? Do they generalize in different topic sets of the same collection? Is performance of our sampling methods different from performance obtained by training on editorial topics and judgments?

System rankings. Are the generated pseudo test collections useful for evaluation purposes, i.e., do they produce similar system rankings as manual collections?

We generate pseudo test collections that use both single annotations and pairs of annotations from the CONTROLLED dimension, and triples of annotations over all three dimensions (i.e., METHOD, CLASSIFICATION, CONTROLLED). In each case, we kept only topics with between a hundred and a thousand documents, resulting in the following numbers of pseudo topics: 2,073, 7,039 and 4,161, respectively. Each of these sampling methods is coupled with two query simulation methods: using keywords and using LLR. Further, we investigate the generalization of our methods by using two topic sets of the GIRT collection, i.e., from 2007, and 2008. This results in 12 experimental conditions.

We evaluate our generated pseudo test collections in two ways: (a) on the retrieval effectiveness of an LTR system, (b) on the similarity of system rankings they produce and system rankings produced on real topics. For the first type of evaluation we use two topic sets, from the CLEF domain specific track: the 2007 topics, and the 2008 topics. We are interested in how training on our pseudo test collections compares to training on real topics. More concretely: How does training on the 2007 topics compare to training on the pseudo test collections when the learned models are tested on the 2008 topics?; and vice versa for the 2008 topics. In addition, we generate two "oracle" runs for each year, namely, an LTR system that trains and tests on the manual topics and assessments in the respective year. For the second type of evaluation on similarity of system ranking, we compare rankings of retrieval systems on manual topics and assessments, and the generated pseudo test collections using Kendall's τ, following [24].

Dataset. We use the collection used in the CLEF domain specific track in 2008 in our experiments. It has two corpora, the GIRT corpus and the CSA SA corpus; for collection statistics see [18].

Learning to rank. For retrieval we use a learning to rank approach. We use a perceptron based algorithm from [19, 20] which was set to optimize performance for the area under the ROC curve. We use two sets of features: (a) query-independent, and (b) query dependent. Table 1 lists 11 query-dependent features (top-half), which are the outputs of off-the-shelf retrieval systems, and 9 query-independent features.

For the query-dependent features we use the Indri, and Terrier retrieval frameworks. For Indri indexing, we use a Porter stemmer, but no stopword removal. For Terrier indexing, we use single-pass indexing, with stopword removal followed by Porter stemming. Both with Indri and Terrier we index all fields, also the keyword field. We normalize features as follows. For the Indri language modeling runs (Indri-LM, Indri-BOW, Indri-BUW, Indri-PRF) we take the exponential of the scores. Then, for each feature, we normalize by dividing by the maximal value for that feature over all documents. In addition to the query dependent features listed in Table 1, we use the query clarity feature by [4].

Our query-independent features include degree-centrality and closeness-centrality. These are properties of nodes in an undirected graph that can be used as measures of influence or centrality in a collaboration network [7]. We calculated them on the co-author graph where nodes are authors and edges exist between authors who co-authored at least one paper, using NetworkX.[2] We assumed that two author fields refer to the same author if and only if the strings match exactly. Query-independent features have values equal to or greater than zero. We normalize each feature by dividing it through its maximal value over all documents.

For our retrieval experiments, we report on average mean precision (MAP). Statistical significance testing is done using Fisher's pairwise randomization test [21], with $\alpha = 0.001$. We use a conservative α level to keep Type I errors under control, as we are making many pairwise comparisons.

---

[2] http://networkx.lanl.gov

Table 1. Query-dependent, and query-independent features for learning to rank. For the features that use properties of authors, we calculate four different values, one based on the first author, and three calculated based on all authors: the maximal, minimal and average value.

Abbr	Description and parameters
Query-dependent features	
Indri-tf-idf	Tf-idf run, with $k_1 = 1.2$ and $b = 0.75$.
Indri-okapi	Okapi BM25 run, with $k_1 = 1.2$, $b = 0.75$, and $k_3 = 7$.
Indri-LM	Language modeling, with Dirichlet smoothing, $\mu = 2500$.
Indri-BOW	LM with boolean ordered window.
Indri-BUW	LM with boolean unordered window.
Indri-PRF	pseudo-relevance feedback(which is based on [13]), we use the 10 top pseudo-relevant documents, we extract 10 terms, we give the original query 0.5 weight and use $\mu = 0$.
Terrier-tf-idf	Tf-idf run, with $k_1 = 1.2$, $b = 0.75$.
Terrier-DFRee	a parameter free DFR (Divergence from Randomness) model.
Terrier-PL2	another DFR run, with $c = 1.0$.
Terrier-QE	a query expansion run, with DFR model Bose-Einstein 1. Query is expanded with the top 10 terms, obtained from the top 3 documents.
Terrier-DSM	a DFR proximity dependence model, with proximity ngram length of 2, $SD = 1$, $FD=1$, and using pBiL. For this model, block indexing has to be performed. We set block.size to 1.
Query-independent features	
docLength	Number of terms in title and abstract.
nAuthors	Number of authors of article.
age	Age of publication (2008 - publication year).
Pubs	Nr. of publications by authors {max,first,avg,min}.
CoAuth	Nr. of co-authors of authors {max,first,avg,min}.
Degree	Degree-centrality of authors {max,first,avg,min}.
Close	Closeness-centrality of authors {max,first,avg,min}.
Pagerank	Pagerank of authors {max,first,avg,min}.

6   Results

Our first experiment aims at answering the question whether training on pseudo test collections leads to different performance from training on editorial test collections. In Table 2 we list performances of our learning to rank algorithm on two sets of queries: the topics (title only) for the 2007 and 2008 editions of the CLEF Domain-Specific track. In the first column it is specified on which topics we train. In the second column the way of obtaining the queries is listed. In the third column we report MAP obtained on the 2007 test topics. We list in boldface the runs that are significantly different from the run that was trained on the 2008 queries. In the last column, MAP on the 2008 topics is given. We list in boldface the runs that differ significantly from the run trained on the 2007

Table 2. MAP performance of our learning to rank approach on the CLEF Domain-Specific 2007 and 2008 topics. ($A_{CONTR.}$ and $A_{CLASSIF.}$ are short for $A_{CONTROLLED}$ and $A_{CLASSIFICATION}$.)

Editorial test collections		
Topics	2007	2008
2008, title only	0.2347	*0.3158*
2007, title only	*0.2226*	0.2970

Pseudo test collections			
Annotations	Query generation	2007	2008
$A_{CONTR.}$	use keywords	**0.1985**	**0.2734**
$A_{CONTR.}$	using LLR	**0.1155**	**0.1869**
$A_{CONTR.} \times A_{CONTR.}$	from keywords	**0.2091**	**0.2866**
$A_{CONTR.} \times A_{CONTR.}$	using LLR	**0.1240**	**0.1959**
$A_{METHOD} \times A_{CLASSIF.} \times A_{CONTR.}$	from keywords	**0.1329**	**0.1609**
$A_{METHOD} \times A_{CLASSIF.} \times A_{CLASSIF.}$	using LLR	**0.1979**	0.2602

data. The two oracle runs—runs that train and test on the same queries—are given in italics.

When we evaluate on the 2008 test topics, we see that three of our six methods of generating a pseudo test collection yield performance that is similar to training on the 2007 test topics: the differences are not statistically significant. This result provides first evidence for the utility of our pseudo test collection generation methods.

Looking at which methods perform well, we see that for $A_{CONTROLLED}$, it is best to use terms occurring in the annotation as query terms, rather than generating a query with LLR, which is worse on both the 2007 and 2008 topics, even though the difference is only significant on the 2007 topics. We observe a similar result for $A_{CONTROLLED} \times A_{CONTROLLED}$; in this case using LLR is significantly worse for both 2007 and 2008. However, for $A_{METHOD} \times A_{CLASSIFICATION} \times A_{CONTROLLED}$, generating the query with LLR is more successful, significantly so for the 2008 topics.

Evaluating on the 2007 test topics yields a different picture. In this case all our methods are significantly outperformed by a learning to rank system trained on the 2008 topics.

We now take a look at the oracle runs. On 2008 test topics, the oracle run is best. Even this run, however, does not improve significantly over $A_{CONTROLLED}$ (using keywords) or $A_{CONTROLLED} \times A_{CONTROLLED}$ (using keywords). It also does not improve significantly over the run that trains on the 2007 topics. On the 2007 test topics, the oracle run is improved by the run that was trained on the 2008 topics, but the difference is not significant. The oracle run obtains a higher score than all our pseudo test collection generation methods, but the differences with $A_{CONTROLLED} \times A_{CONTROLLED}$ and $A_{METHOD} \times A_{CLASSIFICATION} \times A_{CONTROLLED}$ (LLR) are not significant.

6.1   Performance of Individual Features

For completeness, we list scores of our individual features in Table 3, ordered decreasingly by MAP on 2008 topics. The best query-dependent feature is Terrier-QE. However, for 2007, it does not improve significantly over the other Terrier features. Also, with regard to the learning to rank runs: for 2007, it does not significantly outperform the runs that trained on 2008 topics, the 2007 topics, or $A_{CONTROLLED} \times A_{CONTROLLED}$ (using keywords). It is significantly better than all other runs for 2007. For 2008, Terrier-QE does not significantly outperform Indri-tf-idf, nor the other Terrier features. With regard to the learning to rank runs, it does not significantly outperform the runs that train on the 2007 topics, the 2008 topics, or $A_{CONTROLLED}$ (using keywords). All other runs are significantly outperformed.

Some query-dependent feature scores are very high, and even outperform some of our learning to rank approaches. Our main focus is not on showing that we can outperform the best query-dependent feature. Rather, it is to show that we can use pseudo-topics and pseudo-judgments for training with the same effectiveness as editorial topic and judgments.

Table 3. MAP performance of our individual query-dependent features.

Abbr	2007	2008
Indri-tf-idf	0.2028	0.2723
Indri-okapi	0.1821	0.2707
Indri-LM	0.1835	0.2051
Indri-PRF	0.1854	0.1984
Indri-BUW	0.0733	0.1678
Indri-BOW	0.0531	0.1344
Terrier-QE	0.2599	0.3360
Terrier-DFRee	0.2183	0.3107
Terrier-DSM	0.2355	0.3085
Terrier-tf-idf	0.2381	0.2941
Terrier-PL2	0.2277	0.2794

6.2   Using Pseudo Test Collections for Evaluation

In principle, pseudo test collections can be used for evaluation purposes. In Table 4 we list Kendall's tau values between system rankings produced by different test collections. The systems ranked here are the same retrieval algorithms we used for our query dependent features.

Table 4. Kendall's tau values between system rankings produced by different test collections.

	(1)	(2)	(3)	(4)	(5)	(6)	(7)	(8)
(1) 2007	1.000	0.745	0.309	0.294	0.382	0.294	0.636	0.404
(2) 2008		1.000	0.418	0.110	0.564	0.110	0.891	0.220
(3) A_{CT}			1.000	-0.147	0.564	-0.147	0.382	-0.037
(4) A_{CT} (LLR)				1.000	-0.110	0.982	0.000	0.800
(5) $A_{CT} \times A_{CT}$					1.000	-0.110	0.600	0.000
(6) $A_{CT} \times A_{CT}$ (LLR)						1.000	0.000	0.800
(7) $A_M \times A_{CL} \times A_{CT}$							1.000	0.110
(8) $A_M \times A_{CL} \times A_{CT}$ (LLR)								1.000

There is a reasonable correlation between how the 2007 and 2008 topics rank our query-dependent features. The first two rows (and the first two columns) show how all pseudo systems rank systems compared to editorial topics. There are no negative correlations here. It is interesting to note that the pseudo test collection with the strongest correlation with an editorial test collection is $A_M \times A_{CL} \times A_{CT}$; the method that uses documents associated with an annotation triple (METHOD,CLASSIFICATION,CONTROLLED). This is in stark contrast with our previous observation that this pseudo test collection should not be used to train a learning to rank system on.

7 Discussion

We have shown that it is possible to use the rich annotations available in digital libraries collections for training a learning to rank system. We assumed that people annotate documents to make them better findable for certain information needs. We identified three main steps, addressing what kind of annotations to use, how to sample annotations, and how to generate queries. We tackled all three steps and showed that it is possible to generate pseudo test collections in the digital library domain on which a learning to rank system can be trained, such that in some cases performance is indistinguishable from training on editorial topics and judgments. In particular, when testing on the 2008 topics, for three pseudo test collections it holds that training on them yields performance on par with training on 2007 editorial judgments. There is room for improvement with regard to training on the 2008 topics: this strategy outperforms our methods when tested on the 2007 topics.

There are some limitations in our work, which we aim to address in future work. One of them is that our learning to rank algorithm is unable to outperform our best query-dependent feature. We plan to experiment with other learning to rank algorithms and to go beyond using such an algorithm as a black-box.

Another limitation is that we used off-the-shelf retrieval algorithms, and did not tune their parameters. This may limit the quality of our features. It is easy to improve with learning to rank over some of these features, but it is a much harder problem to improve over the best feature. We plan to tune parameters for every query-dependent feature. By tuning them on pseudo test-collections, we can show another way to put pseudo test-collections to good use.

There are some interactions that we do not yet fully understand. One of them is the following. Recall that Asadi et al. [1] sample non-relevant documents from the bottom of a retrieval algorithm ranked list, and we followed this procedure. We chose Indri-LM, but noticed that the choice of algorithm to use has a considerable impact on performance. For example, selecting the Indri-tf-idf algorithm instead of Indri-LM made oracle run performance drop from about MAP 0.30 to MAP 0.25 for 2008 topics. Our choice of the Indri-LM retrieval function was arbitrary, as of yet we have a limited understanding of the properties such a retrieval function should have.

Performance of our query-independent features was also disappointing. The Pegasos [20] algorithm we used for learning to rank learns a linear model, and the weights for all our query-independent features were close to zero. We used 24 document independent features in this paper, but none of them seemed promising enough in a learning to rank setting in order to use them in the query generation process. In future work, we plan to use richer collections which give us the opportunity to test stronger query-independent features based on the citation graph.

8   Conclusion

We have shown that it is feasible to generate pseudo test collections for training a learning to rank system on scientific document collections. We proposed three pseudo test collection generation methods for which we could show that for one of our test sets, training on these collections is just as effective as training on editorial topics and judgments. We pointed to interesting directions for future work and areas where we need to deepen our understanding.

Acknowledgements. This research was partially supported by the European Union's ICT Policy Support Programme as part of the Competitiveness and Innovation Framework Programme, CIP ICT-PSP under grant agreement nr 250430, the European Community's Seventh Framework Programme (FP7/2007-2013) under grant agreements nr 258191 (PROMISE Network of Excellence) and 288024 (LiMoSINe project), the Netherlands Organisation for Scientific Research (NWO) under project nrs 612.061.814, 612.061.815, 640.004.802, 380-70-011, 727.011.005, 612.001.116, the Center for Creation, Content and Technology (CCCT), the Hyperlocal Service Platform project funded by the Service Innovation & ICT program, the WAHSP and BILAND projects funded by the CLARIN-nl program, the Dutch national program COMMIT, and by the ESF Research Network Program ELIAS.

References

[1] Asadi, N., Metzler, D., Elsayed, T., Lin, J.: Pseudo test collections for learning web search ranking functions. In: SIGIR 2011, pp. 1073–1082. ACM (2011)

[2] Azzopardi, L., de Rijke, M., Balog, K.: Building simulated queries for known-item topics: an analysis using six european languages. In: SIGIR 2007, pp. 455–462. ACM (2007)

[3] Beitzel, S., Jensen, E., Chowdhury, A., Grossman, D.: Using titles and category names from editor-driven taxonomies for automatic evaluation. In: CIKM 2003, pp. 17–23. ACM (2003)

[4] Cronen-Townsend, S., Croft, W.: Quantifying query ambiguity. In: HLT 2002, pp. 104–109. Morgan Kaufmann Publishers Inc. (2002)

[5] Di Nunzio, G.M.: Working notes CLEF 2007, Appendix C, Results of the Domain Specific Track. In: Working notes CLEF 2007 (2007)

[6] Di Nunzio, G.M.: Working notes CLEF 2008, Appendix D, Results of the Domain Specific Track. In: Working notes CLEF 2008 (2008)

[7] Easley, D., Kleinberg, J.: Networks, crowds, and markets. Cambridge University Press (2010)

[8] Huurnink, B., Hofmann, K., de Rijke, M.: Simulating searches from transaction logs. In: SIGIR 2010 Workshop on the Simulation of Interaction (2010)

[9] Huurnink, B., Hofmann, K., de Rijke, M., Bron, M.: Validating Query Simulators: An Experiment Using Commercial Searches and Purchases. In: Agosti, M., Ferro, N., Peters, C., de Rijke, M., Smeaton, A. (eds.) CLEF 2010. LNCS, vol. 6360, pp. 40–51. Springer, Heidelberg (2010)

[10] Kim, J., Croft, W.B.: Retrieval experiments using pseudo-desktop collections. In: CIKM 2009, pp. 1297–1306. ACM (2009)

[11] Kluck, M., Gey, F.C.: The Domain-Specific Task of CLEF - Specific Evaluation Strategies in Cross-Language Information Retrieval. In: Peters, C. (ed.) CLEF 2000. LNCS, vol. 2069, pp. 48–56. Springer, Heidelberg (2001)

[12] Kluck, M., Stempfhuber, M.: Domain-Specific Track CLEF 2005: Overview of Results and Approaches, Remarks on the Assessment Analysis. In: Peters, C., Gey, F.C., Gonzalo, J., Müller, H., Jones, G.J.F., Kluck, M., Magnini, B., de Rijke, M., Giampiccolo, D. (eds.) CLEF 2005. LNCS, vol. 4022, pp. 212–221. Springer, Heidelberg (2006)

[13] Lavrenko, V., Croft, W.B.: Relevance based language models. In: SIGIR 2001, pp. 120–127. ACM (2001)

[14] Liu, T.-Y.: Learning to Rank for Information Retrieval. Springer (2011) ISBN 978-3-642-14266-6

[15] Manning, C.D., Schütze, H.: Foundations of statistical natural language processing. MIT Press (1999)

[16] Meij, E., de Rijke, M.: The University of Amsterdam at the CLEF 2008 Domain Specific Track - parsimonious relevance and concept models. In: CLEF 2008 Working Notes (2008)

[17] Petras, V.: How one word can make all the difference - using subject metadata for automatic query expansion and reformulation. In: Working notes CLEF 2005 (2005)

[18] Petras, V.: The domain-specific track at CLEF 2008. In: Working notes CLEF 2008 (2008)

[19] Sculley, D.: Combined regression and ranking. In: KDD 2010, pp. 979–988. ACM (2010)

[20] Shalev-Shwartz, S., Singer, Y., Srebro, N.: Pegasos: Primal estimated sub-gradient solver for SVM. In: 24th International Conference on Machine Learning, pp. 807–814. ACM (2007)

[21] Smucker, M., Allan, J., Carterette, B.: A comparison of statistical significance tests for information retrieval evaluation. In: CIKM 2007, pp. 623–632. ACM (2007)

[22] Tague, J., Nelson, M.: Simulation of user judgments in bibliographic retrieval systems. In: SIGIR 1981, pp. 66–71 (1981)

[23] Tague, J., Nelson, M., Wu, H.: Problems in the simulation of bibliographic retrieval systems. In: SIGIR 1980, pp. 236–255 (1980)

[24] Voorhees, E.M.: Variations in relevance judgments and the measurement of retrieval effectiveness. Information Processing & Management 36(5), 697–716 (2000)

Effects of Language and Topic Size in Patent IR: An Empirical Study

Florina Piroi, Mihai Lupu, and Allan Hanbury

Vienna University of Technology, Vienna, Austria
{piroi,lupu,hanbury}@ifs.tuwien.ac.at

Abstract. We revisit the effects that various characteristics of the topic documents have on the effectiveness of the systems for the task of finding prior art in the patent domain. In doing so, we provide the reader interested in approaching the domain a guide of the issues that need to be addressed in this context.

For the current study, we select two patent based test collections with a common document representation schema and look at topic characteristics specific to the objectives of the collections. We look at the effect of languages on retrieval and at the length of the topic documents. We present the correlations between these topic facets and their retrieval results, as well as their relevant documents.

1 Introduction

The large amounts of available digital information lead to research in large-scale IR engines. This, in turn, brings on questions such as how to evaluate IR engines in a context as realistic as possible. Creating large pools of documents is not a problem, but asking the right questions (topics) and, more importantly, providing the right answers (relevance judgements) is. Efforts to obtain humanly created relevance judgements are done either via a massively distributed online evaluation system (e.g., Amazon's Mechanical Turk webservice [1]), or by re-using specialized work done in some specific contexts [3]. For the data collections in this paper, the latter is the case, as we focus on patent search.

Independent of the tasks organized in an IR evaluation campaign with patent data, the main course in the campaigns of the last decade has been to make proper use of the extremely large amounts of work already done by professional patent searchers worldwide, rather than focusing on consistently reducing the number of topics. Most of the evaluation campaigns using patent data have relevance judgements based on search reports. Although the search report, just like an article's reference list, is never exhaustive, for comparison purposes, the evaluation is still valid and in line with current practice in standard evaluation campaigns. Some caveats in using the search report in this way exist and are specific to the patent domain and the way the intellectual property protection system is designed and functions. They are briefly explained in Section 1.2.

So far, the questions being asked in these evaluation campaigns have been more or less random and give an overview perspective of the performance of different systems. As patent-based test collections mature, we must grasp a better

T. Catarci et al. (Eds.): CLEF 2012, LNCS 7488, pp. 54–66, 2012.

understanding of the characteristics of the topics selected to evaluate systems, and their expected effects on the performance of such systems. Such an analysis can then be used either to act as a baseline (when one knows that, for instance, a particular kind of topic is easily answered by all systems), or to direct future evaluation campaigns into areas where more work is needed to achieve a satisfactory retrieval success.

Prompted by the use of patent search reports as a basis for generating relevance assessments, the CLEF–IP (for Cross-Lingual retrieval) and TREC–CHEM (for chemical retrieval) evaluation campaigns have taken patent application documents and used them as basis for topics in a "prior art" task. The objective: retrieve other patent documents related to the given application.

This study investigates how the results of these evaluation campaigns change when we vary the set of topics based on specific features of the documents used as topics in the evaluation. The scores we observe here are the Mean Average Precision (MAP) and Normalized Discounted Cumulative Gain (NDCG). The document features we take into consideration are: the document language, for the cross-lingual evaluation, and, for both evaluations, the length of the topic documents. While these have been studied to some extent in the literature, it is useful to see to what extent observations made before apply in the context of patent documents. The reasons to believe these observations may be different are as follows:

- most cross-lingual evaluations to date consider the query in one language and the result set in another. Patent retrieval considers the query in one language and the result set in several different languages.
- in the cases where the cross-lingual evaluation task does require a set of results in different language, there is little meta-information that the system can use to connect multilingual documents. In the patent domain, there are several explicit links between documents in different languages (e.g. family membership, inventor, assignee, etc.)
- "verbose" queries in general IR are a few tens or at most hundreds of words. Patent applications, i.e. the topics of prior art search, are thousands, up to hundreds of thousands of words in length and contain different language genres, not commonly found in studies of topical length.

1.1 Outline of the Paper

We continue this section with a compressed introduction to the patenting process, establishing, at the same time, the patent-specific terminology used throughout this paper. Related work on the influence of language and topic sizes, as well as the use of patent collections as IR test collections is described in Section 2. Section 3 describes the four collections used in this study and the methodology for the experiments and ensuing analysis. Section 4 represents the main body of this work, where we look at different aspects of the topic sets selected for this study. We summarize and provide directions for future work in Section 5.

1.2   Brief Survey of Patent Terminology

To facilitate understanding the characteristics of patent-based test collections, we need to establish the terminology used in the patent domain, terminology used throughout this work.

A patent is a set of exclusive legal rights, for a limited period of time, for the use and exploitation of an invention in exchange for its public disclosure. The requirements for granting patents vary among patent offices, but a common first step is to file a patent application request with a patent office. For this, the applicant must supply a written specification of the invention (i.e. a *patent application document*) where the background of the invention, a description of the invention, and a set of claims which define the scope of protection, should the patent be granted, are given. Most of the time, applicants should name (patent) documents relevant to their invention in the text of the application.

To be granted, a patent application is examined by professionals who will analyze whether it meets certain patentability criteria. Of relevance to IR evaluation campaigns is the novelty criteria. A patent application satisfies the novelty requirement if no earlier patent or other kind of publication describing (parts of) the invention can be found in a reasonable amount of time. The search for novelty-relevant documents is called *prior art search*. Results of a prior art search, together with the patents named by the applicants themselves, are recorded in a *search report*. The documents listed in the search report of a patent are referred to as *patent citations* and, at least for European Patent Office (EPO) and Us Patents and Trademarks Office (USPTO), are assigned degrees of relevance, which influence the course of the patent application within its life cycle.

Patent documents generated at the different stages of the patent's life-cycle are identified by a *country code* (denoting the patent office analyzing/granting the patent), a *numeric identifier*, and by a *kind code* together with a version number. Together, these three components form a unique *global* identifier - another very useful feature for IR evaluations.

The main types of patent documents are the ones mentioned above: application document, search report, granted patent. To these, depending on the legal procedures to which a patent is subjected, other patent documents may be added, e.g. additional search reports, documents marking a change in the owner of the invention, countries of applicability, etc. When regarding a patent, all its patent documents must be considered.

To protect an invention in several geographical areas, a patent application can be filed at more than one patent office. When the same invention is granted a patent by different patent offices, the two patents are said to belong to the same *patent family*. In certain conditions, a patent family may contain patents granted by the same patent office. This may happen for instance, when a patent office has a more granular patenting practice, and an invention which was granted one patent by a patent office is split into two or more inventions by another. The use of patent families in IR evaluation is generally useful, as it provides a more complete picture of the set of relevant documents to a topic, but the caveat is that, in situations where a patent application to one patent office is split into several at another, or vice-versa, it is no longer clear which citations are relevant to which of the versions of the same invention.

For the cross-language evaluation campaigns, one feature of the EPO patenting process is of particular interest, namely, the mandatory translations of granted patents. It is a procedural step at the EPO to translate all claims of a granted patent into English, German and French.

2 Related Work

The first retrieval evaluation campaign on a collection of patent documents was organized in the frame of the NTCIR workshop series [5], based on seminal work done in the context of a workshop in 2000 [7].

The NTCIR patent collections contain a significant number of patents, over 3 million in the first year, mostly from the Japanese Patent Office. The tasks and their relevance judgements have changed over the years, including Prior Art, Classification and Machine Translation tasks. After initial experiments with manually evaluated topics, the NTCIR organizers moved to extracting relevance judgments from search reports. Later, in the work done by Fujii et al. [4], relevance judgements obtained from citation records are compared with judgements inferred from patent classification codes, showing considerably different ranking results, but without providing any insight as to which one may be better.

In the past, evaluation campaigns involving cross-language IR have shown various retrieval effectiveness results when looking at the different topic languages (see for example [2],[6] or [15]). Depending on the track settings and the type of data collections involved, retrieval results for English and German topics, for example, were similar [8],[9] or very different [2] with IR systems generally giving a better retrieval efficiency for English topics than other languages.

3 Methodology and Data

The analysis of the results of past evaluation campaigns provide useful insights into common and distinct features of retrieval systems. Existing data can however be overwhelming and difficult to analyze. A clearly defined methodology and target data are identified. The following subsections report on our instantiations.

3.1 Experimental Process

Here are the steps of our methodology, together with explanations and links to the afferent sections.

1. **Initial data selection.** Before starting the process, filter out any parts of the data that cannot be used. This first step must also make sure that the data is large enough for the scope of the analysis. (Section 4.1)

2. **Identification of the investigation subject.** e.g. "How does the language of the topic patent application text influences the rankings and effectiveness measures?" The second step of our working plan identifies the document facets to investigate.
3. **Extract subsets of topics for the investigation subject.** For each of the facets identified above, we divide the entire topic set according to the particular facet under investigation.
4. **Experimentation.** Evaluate the selected retrieval experiments using the subsets. We use `trec_eval`[1] to compute the Mean Average Precision, MAP, and the Normalized Discounted Cumulated Gain, NDCG. In this same computation step we calculate the Kendall's Tau and the Spearman's Rho correlation coefficients between these results and the results using the undivided topic sets. We note here that there are at least two reasons to compute NDCG scores for these test collections: a) the relevance judgements are based on citation reports which have relevance degrees assigned to the relevant documents listed in them; and b) the average number of relevant documents per topic is low compared to other IR tracks.
5. **Analysis.** Observe results, compare to expectations, formulate new hypothesis. We analyze the MAP and NDCG scores and the correlation coefficients and conclude wether the formulated hypotheses are rejected or not. The effects observed on system rankings and retrieval effectiveness are presented in the subsections of Sections 4.2-4.3.

3.2   Test Collections

While consisting of different collections of data, both CLEF–IP and TREC–CHEM had a task named "Prior Art" in 2009 and 2010, where participants were invited to find patent documents in a certain relationship to other (topic) patent documents. Each such topic was phrased as "Please find all patent documents that would potentially invalidate patent X", where X was one of the topic patents. The selection of topics was done depending on the number of patent citations and the source of these citations (applicant, examiner, etc., sources being recorded in the patents' search report documents and available in the data collections).

The extraction of the relevance judgements for these topics was done using the citations, as described in [18], [11]. Characteristic to the patent data is that the number of citations[2] of any given patent is very small compared to the number of relevant documents for a topic in an ad-hoc evaluation campaign. To increase the number of relevant documents per topic, family members of the topic patent and of the citations were also included in the relevance judgements. By this procedure, for the set of CLEF–IP 09 topics in this study, the average number of relevant documents per topic was raised from 1.89 to 5.63, while for the TREC–CHEM 09 collection the average number of relevant document per

---

[1] http://trec.nist.gov/trec_eval/trec_eval_latest.tar.gz
[2] Recall that a patent *citation* refers to a document that is relevant to the patent.

topics increased from 30.8 to 48.9. Previous work [10] has shown that citation-based relevance judgments are indeed closer, in terms of ranking correlation, to manual judgments than fully automatic pseudo-judgments.

CLEF–IP 2009/2010 The CLEF–IP test collection is the first collection of patents with content in three main European languages addressed to the evaluation of cross-lingual IR. The patents are obtained from the EPO and contain text in German, English, and French [18]. The documents are assigned a 'document language', but parts of their content may additionally occur in one or both of the other languages. The documents in the collections refer to over 1, respectively 1.3 million patents published before the year 2000 (CLEF–IP 09) and 2001 (CLEF–IP 10). In both years the topics were extracted from a pool of documents different from the distributed corpus, a pool which contained over 0.7 million patent documents published after the documents in the corpus.

The Prior Art Search task organized in 2009 had a very large number of topics (10000). The topics were syntetic documents, created such that at least the claims were available in all 3 languages in the collection [18]. In 2010 the number of topics was reduced to 2000, the topic documents were patent application documents with the claims usually present in one language only [16].

TREC–CHEM 2009/2010 The TREC–CHEM test collection has been used for the Chemical IR track of TREC [19]. It contains both patent documents and scientific articles, all chemistry-related. The task of interest for us in this article, the Prior Art Task, used only a subset with 1.1 million patent documents that contained claims and either an abstract or a description of the invention, or both. The documents are obtained from the USPTO and the EPO.

The 2010 version of the collection has added more content to the scientific articles sub-collection, and added a set of images and chemical structure files to the collection. For the prior art task, the patent sub-collection was increased to approximately 1.3 million documents, not only from the USPTO and EPO sources, but also from the World Intellectual Property Organization (WIPO).

Each TREC–CHEM 2009 and 2010 contained a set of 1,000 topics for the Prior Art Search task.

4 Analysis

In this section we instantiate the methodology described in Section 3.1. We want to examine whether the observations made in other retrieval contexts with respect to the influence of language and size of the topic apply in the case of patents. We look at these two aspects in sections 4.2 and 4.3, respectively. For each of them, we outline the lessons learned for both participants and evaluation campaign organizers.

4.1 Selecting the Data

For the purpose of this study, we have used the same topic sets as the evaluation campaigns in the case of the TREC–CHEM collections. In the CLEF–IP case we chose a random subset of 1,000 topics out of the largest set of topics in 2009 (10,000), and 1937 topics out of 2000 topics in 2010 (it was later found that 63 topics had faulty relevance judgements).

To test our hypotheses we have made evaluations on experiments submitted to the two campaigns. The evaluation results described in this section are obtained by evaluating the data in 15 runs of the TREC–CHEM09 track, 9 runs of TREC–CHEM10, 24 runs of CLEF–IP09, and 18 of the CLEF–IP10 track for the above mentioned sets of topics, respectively. Although the number of submissions to both tracks is larger, we selected only the runs that actually provide results for all of the topics in each set.

4.2   The 'Document Language' Feature

When examining a patent application for the novelty criteria a patent professional has to look for prior art in all collections available to her, regardless of language. It is often the case that for a patent application written in, for example, German there are relevant documents written in English or French. The CLEF–IP collection includes these cases, and since the collection was meant for cross-language retrieval, it is expected to look at how the topic's document language reflect upon the retrieval results.

We split each of the CLEF–IP topic sets in this study in three, based on the document language. For both years, approximately 60% of the topics have the document language English, 30% German, and 10% French. (This distribution faithfully reflects the distribution of document language in the whole CLEF–IP collection.)

Effects On System Rankings and Effectiveness Measures. We have computed the MAP and NDCG scores (not displayed here) and the correlation coefficients between the system rankings (Table 1).

As it can be seen, the rankings are generally highly correlated. The lower correlation scores for the German language, the most different of the three, due to its compounding, reflect the fact that experiments which did not take this into account suffered a significant drop in performance. Regarding the MAP (highest values 0.35 in 2009, 0.38 in 2010) and NDCG (highest values 0.57 in 2010, 0.54 in 2009) scores we have found that about half of the runs were better in finding documents for English language topics, the other half is better for the German ones, while French topics get the lowest scores for almost all runs. This is due to the various and particular methods that the participating systems involved to treat the multilingual aspect of the CLEF–IP data collection (see [17] Appendix). For CLEF–IP as for other cross-language retrieval tasks, the language issue is not only to differently treat the documents with different languages, but also to care for the language difference between topic documents and relevant documents. To analyse how well this was done, we split the two sets of topics into difficulty bins based on the number of experiments that retrieved their relevant documents. To each relevant document of a topic T is assigned a score equal to the number of

Table 1. Correlations of language based topic subsets with the full topic set in CLEF–IP

	CLEF–IP09				CLEF–IP10			
	MAP		NDCG		MAP		NDCG	
	τ	ρ	τ	ρ	τ	ρ	τ	ρ
EN	0.79	0.88	0.79	0.91	0.93	0.98	0.93	0.97
DE	0.6	0.8	0.64	0.82	0.90	0.96	0.78	0.81
FR	0.69	0.84	0.69	0.87	0.96	0.99	0.78	0.78

experiments that retrieved it. The topic T is in the difficulty bin b_j when the median of its relevant documents scores is j.

Fig. 1 shows the number of topics in each bin, and the percentages of relevant documents having the same document language as the topic document. It is easy to see from the two figures that the fewer relevant documents with a different document language than the topic's, the more systems are able to find them.

Surprisingly, there are no topics in bins b_0 to b_{11} for CLEF–IP 2009, which means that at least 12 runs have found most of the relevant documents for all the 1000 selected topics for this study. One reason behind this is that different type of judgements were provided: in 2009 the relevance judgements were at the patent level, while in 2010 they were given at patent *document* level. The effect of this is that in 2009 more patents were returned as relevant compared to the 2010 results when looking at patents and not patent documents[3]. The second reason behind empty bins is to be found in differences in the origins of the topic document for the two campaign years [18], [16]. The 2009 topic files were artificially created to have a large amount of replicated content in three languages, which made the cross-lingual retrieval problem easier by using monolingual searches.

We note, though, that the margin bins, b_{12} and b_{24} in 2009, and b_1 and b_{18} in 2010 could be joined into their next neighboring bins, as they contain too few topics to draw any believable conclusion.

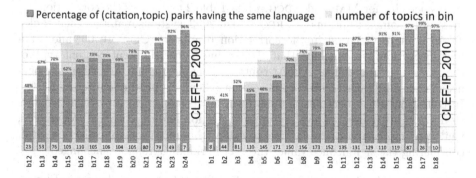

Fig. 1. Language as a sources of difficulty in topics, CLEF–IP 09 and CLEF–IP 10

---

[3] See section 1.2 for the difference between patents and patent documents.

Lessons Learned. The results we have seen while looking at the effect of the document language on IR scores confirm the research published in the CLIR tracks at TREC[4] or CLEF[5] related papers.

In the case of the CLEF–IP track, the better scores for the English topics are most likely due to the English documents being over-represented in the target collection. This makes it such that even systems that effectively discarded non-English document were able to obtain good scores.

We do remark, though, that the top ranking runs performed better for non-English than for English topics. This is to be attributed to the use of further patent specific data and patent expert know-how in the respective retrieval experiments. This pleads in favor of at least augmenting 'off-the-shelf' retrieval solutions with implementations of patent specific know–how in order to obtain IR systems that better perform in a setting like CLEF–IP.

Participants must be aware that without specific language processing, they will not reach the best scores.

4.3   The 'Document Size' Feature

In general IR, it is common knowledge that a longer narrative is easier to answer and evaluate, therefore systems tend to perform better. We ask whether this is still the case in the patent domain, where longer documents are usually associated with having a verbose, legal document—not necessarily useful for retrieval.

In order to observe potential differences, we have divided the TREC–CHEM and CLEF–IP topics into 10 bins of equal sizes, based on their number of words. In the ascending order of their word count, bin 1 contains 10% of the topics with the fewest words, bin 2 the next 10% more verbose topics, and so on until bin 10 which contains the top 10% most verbose topics. Each bin contains 100 topic documents, with all but one CLEF–IP2010 bins containing 193 topics, the last one containing 200 topics.

Effects on System Rankings. Figures 2 to 5 show the different (average) scores per bins for MAP and NDCG, while Table 2 and shows the correlation figures. With some exceptions in TREC–CHEM 2009, systems maintain their ranks. There is more variation in the correlation results for CLEF–IP 09, and, at a first inspection, we conclude that this is due to the different content type of the two collections. TREC–CHEM contains documents that are more homogeneous regarding their technological content (chemistry) compared to the CLEF–IP collection which contains patents from all technological areas. Participants to TREC–CHEM use retrieval systems tuned for finding chemical documents, while participants to CLEF–IP have to deal with a more general collection. Still, considering the significance values the overall rankings remain unchanged.

Effects on Effectiveness Measures. For TREC–CHEM, we observe in Figures 2 and 3 that MAP and NDCG do tend to be higher for bins of topics with higher

---

[4] http://trec.nist.gov
[5] http://www.clef.org

Table 2. Correlations for subsets of topics based on the size of the topics

bin	TREC–CHEM09 MAP τ	ρ	NDCG τ	ρ	TREC–CHEM10 MAP τ	ρ	NDCG τ	ρ	CLEF–IP09 MAP τ	ρ	NDCG τ	ρ	CLEF–IP10 MAP τ	ρ	NDCG τ	ρ
1	0.85	0.96	0.90	0.97	0.83	0.93	1.0	1.0	0.68	0.83	0.69	0.84	0.92	0.98	099	1.0
2	0.83	0.95	0.89	0.98	0.89	0.97	1.0	1.0	0.6	0.75	0.67	0.85	0.99	1.0	0.96	0.99
3	0.94	0.99	0.98	1.0	0.89	0.95	1.0	1.0	0.69	0.84	0.84	0.93	0.99	1.0	0.97	1.0
4	0.94	0.99	1.0	1.0	0.89	0.97	1.0	1.0	0.9	0.92	0.9	0.98	0.89	0.97	1.0	1.0
5	0.98	1.0	1.0	1.0	0.89	0.95	0.94	0.98	0.75	0.88	0.82	0.94	0.91	0.97	0.95	0.98
6	0.94	0.98	0.94	0.99	0.94	0.98	1.0	1.0	0.65	0.8	0.78	0.93	0.93	0.98	0.93	0.99
7	0.94	0.98	0.92	0.98	0.89	0.97	1.0	1.0	0.63	0.79	0.67	0.84	0.84	0.91	0.84	0.91
8	0.89	0.95	0.90	0.98	1.0	1.0	0.89	0.97	0.67	0.84	0.75	0.9	0.71	0.83	0.82	0.91
9	0.81	0.92	0.89	0.97	0.94	0.98	0.83	0.93	0.71	0.84	0.73	0.88	0.69	0.83	0.7	0.79
10	0.71	0.85	0.83	0.93	0.89	0.97	0.83	0.93	0.72	0.88	0.8	0.9	0.83	0.89	0.75	0.79

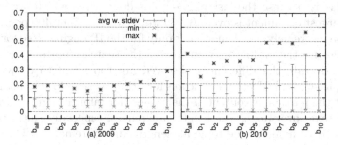

Fig. 2. TREC–CHEM MAP results for topic subsets based on the size of the topics

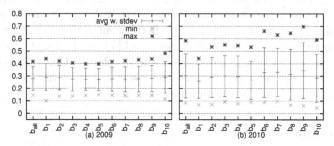

Fig. 3. TREC–CHEM NDCG results for topic subsets based on the size of the topics

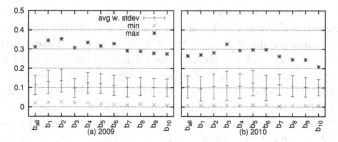

Fig. 4. CLEF–IP MAP results for topic subsets based on the size of the topics

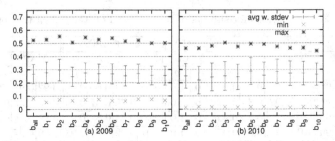

Fig. 5. CLEF–IP NDCG results for topic subsets based on the size of the topics

word counts. This is particularly so for the systems which perform better also on average, as they are able to properly process the input documents and extract the necessary query terms. In 2010, the trend of increasing performance with the increase of the topic size stops at the second last bin (b_9), which is not the case in 2009. This is because the last bin contains documents which are extremely large (the largest document is over 400000 words long—about 400 pages of text) and therefore extremely problematic not only for the IR engines (see for example [12]), but also for the evaluators who created the search reports.

However, overall, the differences observed are too small to draw any link between topic size and effectiveness scores for prior-art search. It appears that in this context the particular content of the request for information (i.e. the patent application text) overweighs the length differences, especially since, compared to standard IR campaigns, the topic file lengths are extreme.

Lessons Learned. The size of the topic document is not an as important factor for this task as it is for information retrieval in general. It is not the case that longer or shorter topics perform better, but rather that extreme topic sizes perform worse. Therefore, such cases should either be handled separately, or methods aware of extreme cases should be developed. Campaign organisers must make sure that all topic sizes are represented in the test collection, not necessarily following any distribution in the corpora.

5   Conclusion

Although it is known that the disclosures made in published patents constitute a large corpus of technological know-how and development, patent data is hardly used in a researcher's work. A main reasons for this is that scientists in the academic communities find it difficult to retrieve data out of patent repositories. Evaluation campaigns that use patents are an important step in bringing this kind of data closer to the them. They incite research about how IR methods perform on this data. The present work contributes to this research focus.

In general terms, this study illustrates how topic feature analysis can be done in the context of a test collection. To this end we have designed a methodology which we apply to revisit some of the observations made in a general IR context, for two patent-based test collections.

In the case of the multilingual collections, we found that while English queries tend to perform, on average, marginally better when considering all runs, the system rankings are sensitive to the use of a different language in the query. Still, patent know-how is a deciding factor in the performance of a system, able to overweight the cross-lingual deficiencies of the system. Another hypothesis, that documents with more text tend to perform better on average, could not be verified. The topic length also did not change the ranking of the systems.

A further analysis of other document characteristics in the patent domain would be useful, and the decision as to which of the many potential facets of the documents should be investigated lies with the organizers of such evaluation campaigns, as a function of the target audience (both in terms of participants and end-users).

References

1. Alonso, O., Mizzaro, S.: Can we get rid of TREC assessors? Using Mechanical Turk for relevance assessment. In: Proc. of SIGIR IR Evaluation Workshop (2009)
2. Ferro, N., Peters, C.: CLEF 2009 Ad Hoc Track Overview: TEL and Persian Tasks. In: Peters et al. [14]
3. Fujii, A.: Enhancing patent retrieval by citation analysis. In: Proc. of SIGIR (2007)
4. Fujii, A., Iwayama, M., Kando, N.: Overview of the Patent Retrieval Task at the NTCIR-6 Workshop. In: Proc. of EVIA (2007)
5. Iwayama, M., Fujii, A., Kando, N., Takano, A.: Report on the patent retrieval task at NTCIR workshop 3. SIGIR Forum 38(1), 22–24 (2004)
6. Kishida, K., Chen, K.-H., Lee, S., Kuriyama, K., Kando, N., Chen, H.-H., Myaeng, S.H., Eguchi, K.: Overview of CLIR Task at the Fourth NTCIR Workshop. In: Proc. of the NTCIR Workshop (2004)
7. Kando, N., Leong, M.-K.: Workshop on Patent Retrieval (Workshop Report). SIGIR Forum 34(1) (2000)
8. Kürsten, J., Wilhelm, T., Eibl, M.: The Xtrieval Framework at CLEF 2008: Domain-Specific Track. In: Peters, et al. [13]
9. Larson, R.: Back to Basics - Again - for Domain-Specific Retrieval. In: Peters et al. [13]
10. Lupu, M., Piroi, F., Hanbury, A.: Aspects and analysis of patent test collections. In: Proc. of PaIR (2010)
11. Lupu, M., Piroi, F., Huang, J., Zhu, J., Tait, J.: Overview of the TREC Chemical IR Track. In: Proc. of the 18th Text Retrieval Conference (2010)
12. Lv, Y., Zhai, C.: When documents are very long, BM25 fails! In: Proc. of SIGIR (2011)
13. Peters, C., Deselaers, T., Ferro, N., Gonzalo, J., Jones, G.J.F., Kurimo, M., Mandl, T., Peñas, A., Petras, V. (eds.): CLEF 2008. LNCS, vol. 5706. Springer, Heidelberg (2009)
14. Peters, C., Di Nunzio, G.M., Kurimo, M., Mandl, T., Mostefa, D., Peñas, A., Roda, G. (eds.): CLEF 2009. LNCS, vol. 6241. Springer, Heidelberg (2010)
15. Petras, V., Baerisch, S.: The Domain-Specific Track at CLEF 2008. In: Peters et al. [13]

16. Piroi, F.: CLEF-IP 2010: Retrieval Experiments in the Intellectual Property Domain. In: CLEF 2010 LABs and Workshops, Notebook Papers (2010)
17. Piroi, F., Zenz, V.: Evaluating Information Retrieval in the Intellectual Property Domain: The CLEF-IP Campaign. In: Current Challenges in Patent Information Retrieval. The Information Retrieval Series, vol. 29 (2011)
18. Roda, G., Tait, J., Piroi, F., Zenz, V.: CLEF-IP 2009: Retrieval Experiments in the Intellectual Property Domain. In: Peters et al. [14]
19. Voorhees, E., Buckland, L. (eds.): Proc. of TREC, volume Special Publication 500–278. NIST (2009)

Cross-Language High Similarity Search
Using a Conceptual Thesaurus

Parth Gupta, Alberto Barrón-Cedeño, and Paolo Rosso

Natural Language Engineering Lab. - ELiRF
Department of Information Systems and Computation
Universitat Politècnica de València, Spain
{pgupta,lbarron,prosso}@dsic.upv.es
http://www.dsic.upv.es/grupos/nle

Abstract. This work addresses the issue of cross-language high similarity and near-duplicates search, where, for the given document, a highly similar one is to be identified from a large cross-language collection of documents. We propose a concept-based similarity model for the problem which is very light in computation and memory. We evaluate the model on three corpora of different nature and two language pairs English-German and English-Spanish using the Eurovoc conceptual thesaurus. Our model is compared with two state-of-the-art models and we find, though the proposed model is very generic, it produces competitive results and is significantly stable and consistent across the corpora.

1 Introduction

The task of high similarity search refers to the identification of documents that are duplicates or share almost identical information. The proliferation of information in the age of the Web is extremely high and there exists a large redundancy in the contents of newly generated text. High similarity search becomes important either to avoid or to exploit redundancy. The former refers to the technology of duplicate identification for Web search indexing, also known as near-duplicate detection; whereas the latter corresponds to high similarity search for text classification, document clustering, plagiarism detection and retrieval by example. This problem is well studied for the monolingual variant and the most popular approaches are related to shingling [1], and the majority of research is based on the selection of a representative signature for the documents in question [2,3,4].

Documents with similar content also exist across languages, e.g. Wikipedia articles in multiple languages, news stories in different languages covering the same event, cross-language cases of plagiarism, and translated documents. Identification of such documents across languages is also referred as cross-language (CL) high similarity search, CL near-duplicate identification and CL pairwise similarity in the literature, but has attained less attention compared to its monolingual counterpart [5,6].

Usually, in this framework the length of the query is quite large (i.e. a whole document). Although it induces more information for the similarity estimation, this may potentially introduce noise. Moreover, the CL setting, where one term in language L_1

T. Catarci et al. (Eds.): CLEF 2012, LNCS 7488, pp. 67–75, 2012.

may stand equivalent to many completely different terms in language L_2, in addition to a large reference collection, introduces a new twist in the problem. The large vocabulary of the collection is *dangerous* in terms of ambiguity and computational cost.

We propose an algorithm which measures the CL similarity based on a conceptual thesaurus (CT). The main contributions of this work are twofold:

1. A method to represent documents (of any domain) in the conceptual space using a domain specific CT is suggested.
2. A novel method for CL high similarity search based on a reduced vocabulary (concepts) is proposed.

The rest of the paper is structured as follows. In Section 2, we present the related work. Section 3 describes the CT used and the models in detail. In Section 4, we present the performance evaluation of the approach and analysis. Finally, in Section 5 we summarise the work.

2   Related Work

Recently, there have been many attempts to address the issue of CL high similarity search. Anderka et al. [5] discuss the fact that, linear scan is inevitable for CL high similarity search, empirically and theoretically but do not report experimental results of the actual retrieval. Ture et al. [6] report the results of locality-sensitive hashing scheme [1] for the specified problem using MapReduce [7] and conclude as no optimal solution to reduce the search space. Moreover, they concentrate more on the scalability issues of the problem. In another approach, Platt et al. [8] suggest an oriented principle component analysis (OPCA) based learning in which multilingual documents are represented in a common space, but as they further mention, this technique is impractical for large vocabularies because the temporal and spatial cost scale quadratically with the vocabulary size.

Eurovoc has previously been used for the identification of translated documents [9,10], in which, the Eurovoc concepts were enriched by a set of associative phrases extracted from a large manually (keywords) annotated corpus. The Eurovoc concepts are then assigned to the documents based on the similarity between the contents of the document and the enriched associative set. This approach is quite restrictive because it demands a large manually annotated and domain dependent corpora for the association of Eurovoc concepts to the documents.

The CL explicit semantic analysis model (CL-ESA) tries to estimate the semantic similarity between two documents based on a comparable corpus [11]. The CL alignment based similarity analysis model (CL-ASA) is an adaptation of IBM M1 [12], in which the translation model is adapted to handle long texts and the language model is substituted by a length model [9] to measure the similarity [13,14]. Another model is based on the comparison of character n-grams (CL-CNG) between the documents [15]. Recently, these three models were compared in [16]. CL-ASA and CNG showed better performance on different corpora like JRC and Wikipedia. Therefore, we compare the proposed model with CL-ASA and CL-CNG.

3 Models

In this Section we describe our proposed model as well as the models we compare it with. The proposed model tries to measure the similarity between the documents in terms of shared concepts, assigned using a CT, and named entities (NEs) among them.

3.1 Conceptual Thesaurus

A CT contains concepts that are often multi-word structures and exhaustively try to cover the omnipresent concepts of the specific domain. The CT we use is Eurovoc[1], which has emerged from European Parliamentary proceedings. Eurovoc is a thriving resource and contains 6,797 multilingual concepts maintained with comparable identifiers (*concept id*) in 22 languages, which span across 21 domains of European Parliament activities. Some of the entries of Eurovoc are presented in Table 1.

Table 1. Examples of Eurovoc descriptors in the three languages

English	Spanish	German
action for failure to fulfil an obligation	recurso por incumplimiento	Klage wegen Vertragsverletzung
extra-community trade	intercambio extracomunitario	außergemeinschaftlicher Handel
sexual harassment	acoso sexual	sexuelle Belästigung

3.2 Cross-Language Conceptual Thesaurus Based Similarity (CL-CTS)

We represent the documents as a vector of the concepts in the thesaurus, rather than the original terms of the document. Concept assignment is the least trivial part. The concept assignment based on its verbatim occurrence in the document produces poor results [17]. Therefore, we assign a concept to a document if it "triggers the concept". Triggering is explained by the function $v(e, d)$ where e and d are Eurovoc concept and reference document respectively:

$$v(e, d) = \sum_{t \in e, T_e} f(t, d) \qquad (1)$$

where, $f(t, d)$ depicts the frequency of term t in d. $\forall t \in e \cup d$ is stemmed and not a stopword. T_e refers to the vocabulary of Eurovoc concepts. The concept e is assigned to d with weight $v(e, d)$ if $v(e, d) > 0$.

We try to exploit this multilingual structure based on a heuristic: *the terms together are highly domain dependent but alone are domain independent*, e.g. "community" and "trade" may individually well be present in any domain compared to the complete descriptor "community trade". Moreover, we believe not all the terms help in the similarity estimation. Fig. 1 depicts the document frequency (*df*) of Eurovoc concept terms T_e,

---

[1] http://eurovoc.europa.eu/

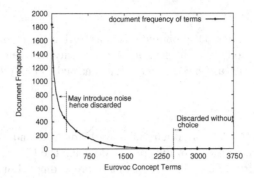

Fig. 1. Document frequency (in decreasing order) of the Eurovoc concept terms in the PAN sub-corpus (cf. Section 4.1)

which is well in accordance with the Zipf's law. $\forall t \in T_e$, $df(t) = 0$ specifies that t does not participate in the similarity estimation. On the other hand, there are few terms for which, $df(t)$ is very high. These terms are less discriminative and, more importantly, very likely to introduce noise by increasing the similarity of non-relevant documents, especially when we use a reduced vocabulary. Therefore, we choose $t \in T_e$ for which $0 < df(t) < \beta$ as T'_e which is referred as reduced concepts (RC). In case of RC, T_e is replaced by T'_e in Eq. 1.

The conceptual vectors representing the documents are constructed on a monolingual basis, where each dimension represents one *concept id*. To find the similar documents for a given document q in language L_1, from the collection of documents D in language L_2, similarity between the conceptual vectors of q and $\forall d \in D$ is calculated as in Eq. 2, where c corresponds to the conceptual vector and $|\cdot|$ denotes *cardinality*.

$$\omega(q,d) = \frac{\alpha}{2} * \left(\frac{c_q \cdot c_d}{|q||d|} + \ell(q,d) \right) + (1-\alpha) * \zeta(q,d) \qquad (2)$$

The first term is the conceptual component and the second is the named entity (NE) component. Here, $\zeta(\cdot, \cdot)$ defines the cosine similarity of char 3-grams between the NEs, $\ell(\cdot, \cdot)$ is the length factor (LF) penalty for the document pair as defined in [9] and α is the weighing factor so that $\omega(q,d) \in [0,1]$. The motivation behind the NE component is, NEs act as the discriminative features for the identification of different documents on the similar conceptual topics. To handle the variation of NEs across languages, we use character n-gram based similarity estimation. Moreover, the parallel documents follow a specific length distributions as specified in [9] that helps in incorporating the length information of parallel document pairs. Inclusion of LF induces this information in the similarity estimation.

3.3 Cross-Language Alignment Based Similarity Analysis (CL-ASA)

CL-ASA measures the similarity between two documents from different languages by estimating the likelihood of one document being a translation of the other one [13,14]. The similarity between the documents q and $d \in D$ is computed as in Eq. 3.

$$\omega(q,d) = \ell(q,d) * t(q \mid d) \qquad (3)$$

where, $\ell(q,d)$ is again the length factor defined in [9] and the translation model $t(q \mid d)$ is calculated as in Eq. 4.

$$t(q \mid d) = \sum_{x \in q} \sum_{y \in d} p(x,y) \qquad (4)$$

where, $p(x,y)$ is computed on the basis of a statistical bilingual dictionary which can be obtained from a parallel corpus.

3.4   Cross-Language Character n-Grams (CL-CNG)

The character n-grams have shown to improve the performance of cross-language information retrieval immensely for syntactically similar languages [15]. The documents are codified into the space of character n-grams and represented as the vectors of them. The CL-CNG measures the $\omega(q,d)$ as shown in Eq. 5.

$$\omega(q,d) = \frac{q' \cdot d'}{|q'||d'|} \qquad (5)$$

where q' and d' are the projected vectors of q and d into character n-grams space.

4   Experiments and Analysis

We consider the documents in English as query documents $q \in Q$ and the documents in German or Spanish as reference documents $d \in D$. The aim is to find the highly similar document d for each q from D for each source language. In our experimental set up, there exists a highly similar document $d \in D$ for each q and the performance of the algorithms is evaluated in terms of the retrieval quality. We carry out the evaluation of the algorithms on three different datasets (Section 4.1) and two language pairs: English-Spanish (en-es) and English-German (en-de). We compare the proposed model with two state-of-the-art models, CL-ASA and CL-CNG. The results and analysis are presented in Sections 4.2 and 4.3 respectively.

4.1   Datasets

We extracted a collection of parallel documents from the JRC-Acqis corpus[2] referred as JRC, CL plagiarism cases from the PAN-PC-11 corpus[3] referred as PAN and Wikipedia comparable articles referred as Wiki for both language pairs. The JRC sub-corpus amounts to 10,000 documents for each language, PAN sub-corpus contains 2920 en-es and 2222 en-de document pairs and Wiki sub-corpus contains 10,000 documents for each language. The partitions of the JRC-Acquis and Wikipedia sub-collections

---

[2] http://optima.jrc.it/Acquis/
[3] http://www.uni-weimar.de/cms/medien/webis/
research/corpora/pan-pc-11.html

used in the experiments are publicly available[4]. Our complete test collection includes 70,282 documents. The JRC corpus contains documents related to European Commission activities, while the PAN sub-corpus contains documents from Project Gutenberg[5]. Therefore, the vocabulary shared by Eurovoc and JRC is higher than that of Eurovoc and PAN or Wiki.

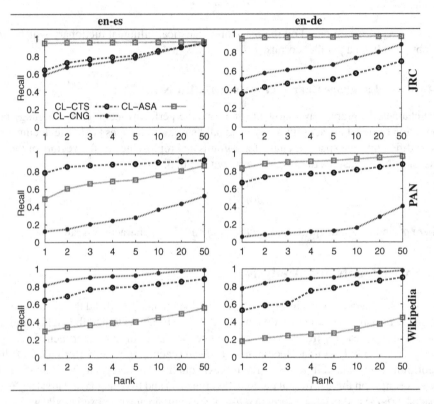

Fig. 2. Results of the proposed CL-CTS model on the JRC, PAN and Wiki sub-corpora and comparison with CL-CNG and CL-ASA. The performace is evaluated as Recall-over-Rank, where Recall@1 refers to the identification of the highly similar document at the very first position in the ranklist.

4.2 Results

We trained the translation model of CL-ASA on a different partition of JRC corpus of 10,000 parallel documents for each language pair and length factor values are used as suggested in [16]. The diacritics of Spanish and German are normalised for the similarity estimation in case of CL-CNG and n=3 is used. The parameters of CL-CTS, α and β, were set empirically on a small validation set of 500 documents from each corpus. We used $\beta = 0.10*|D|$ for the three corpora while the $\alpha = 0.95$ for the JRC and $\alpha=0.50$

[4] http://users.dsic.upv.es/grupos/nle/downloads.html
[5] http://www.gutenberg.org/

for the PAN and Wiki. Moreover, the LF is disabled on Wiki sub-corpus as the documents are not parallel. The performance of the models is measured by recall-over-rank as depicted in Fig. 2.

4.3 Analysis

The performance of CL-CTS with reduced concepts is much higher compared to the inclusion of all concepts because including the very common concepts increases the similarity score of some irrelevant documents. Let T'_{e,L_1} and T'_{e,L_2} denote the Eurovoc reduced concepts for language L_1 and L_2 respectively. The performance with RC heuristic will be driven by the size of $|T'_{e,L_1} \cap T'_{e,L_2}|$, which is usually quite high for parallel and comparable corpora, where $| \cdot \cap \cdot | = 1$ if both sets contain equivalent CT concepts in the respective languages. In general, the incorporation of NE component improves the performance except for JRC, which is very biased towards a particular category of NE as discussed later in this section. But this effect was minimised by the value of $\alpha = 0.95$ for JRC. To handle the terms compounding in German we used jWordSplitter[6] which employs a greedy approach for splitting. Usually, German document retrieval stays more difficult compared to Spanish document retrieval for the word-based approaches because of the terms compounding.

Table 2. Average distribution of NEs in the three corpora

Corpus	Person	Location	Organisation	Total
JRC	1.8%	2.3%	8.7%	12.9%
PAN	1.8%	1.7%	1.9%	5.4%
Wiki	4.7%	3.7%	5.5%	14.0%

The other systems, CL-CNG and CL-ASA show very corpus dependent performance. To better describe this behaviour, we present the nature of these corpora and some statistics of the named entities[7] in the corpora in Table 2. JRC contains *parallel* documents of the European Commission activities which are highly domain dependent and contain quite large amount of NEs of type Organisation and Location (country names). These names appear quite identically in several documents. PAN contains cross-language plagiarism cases, which can be treated as *noisy parallel* data. These documents were generated using the machine translation technologies to translate text fragments from Project Gutenberg documents [16]. PAN documents are about literature and contain far more natural language terms compared to NEs. On the other hand, Wikipedia articles are *comparable* documents with a high amount of NEs. The amount and type of NEs in PAN and Wiki are quite diverse and balanced compared to JRC.

CL-ASA performs better on the JRC sub-corpus and very poor on the Wiki sub-corpus while CL-CNG performs better on the Wiki sub-corpus and very poor on the PAN sub-corpus. CL-ASA produces better results on nearly parallel data while CL-CNG demonstrates better performance on the NE dominated corpora. CL-CTS exhibits

---

[6] http://www.danielnaber.de/jwordsplitter/
[7] LingPipe NE Recogniser is used for English and Spanish; while, Stanford NER for German.

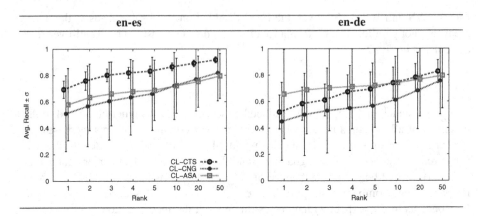

Fig. 3. Mean and standard deviation of the performance of the algorithms over different corpora

very stable performance across the corpora. The average performance of all the systems with their standard deviation is shown in Fig. 3. It is noticeable from the standard deviation values that CL-CTS is the most consistent across the corpora. CL-CTS can be very useful in the situation when the nature of the data is unknown or when dealing with a heterogeneous data. Moreover, CL-CTS uses a reduced vocabulary equals to $|T_e'|$ and NEs to measure the similarity between q and d. Other terms are discarded, resulting in very compact inverted index and a low computational cost. This reduces the temporal and spatial cost of the model dramatically. It should also be noted that CL-CTS achieves a stable performance across the domain with a domain specific conceptual thesaurus.

5   Summary and Future Work

We have proposed a model based on conceptual similarity for cross-language high similarity search which has very low temporal and spatial cost. The proposed model outperforms the character n-gram similarity based model on the linguistic sub-corpus PAN. The model also outperforms the machine translation based model on the comparable Wikipedia sub-corpus. The model demonstrates a very high stability across the corpora and performs consistently.

In future, we plan to test this model on a wide variety of language pairs, such as English with Hindi, Greek and Arabic. We also plan to compare the performance of this model to statistical conceptual models such as latent semantic analysis.

Acknowledgment. This work was done in the framework of the VLC/CAMPUS Microcluster on Multimodal Interaction in Intelligent Systems and it has been partially funded by the European Commission as part of the WIQ-EI IRSES project (grant no. 269180) within the FP 7 Marie Curie People Framework, and by the Text-Enterprise 2.0 research project (TIN2009-13391-C04-03). The research work of the second author is supported by the CONACyT 192021/302009 grant.

References

1. Broder, A.Z.: Identifying and Filtering Near-Duplicate Documents. In: Giancarlo, R., Sankoff, D. (eds.) CPM 2000. LNCS, vol. 1848, pp. 1–10. Springer, Heidelberg (2000)
2. Chowdhury, A., Frieder, O., Grossman, D., McCabe, M.C.: Collection Statistics for Fast Duplicate Document Detection. ACM Trans. Inf. Syst. 20, 171–191 (2002)
3. Charikar, M.S.: Similarity Estimation Techniques from Rounding Algorithms. In: Proceedings of the Thiry-fourth Annual ACM Symposium on Theory of Computing, STOC 2002, pp. 380–388. ACM, New York (2002)
4. Kolcz, A., Chowdhury, A., Alspector, J.: Improved Robustness of Signature-based Near-Replica Detection via Lexicon Randomization. In: Proceedings of the Tenth ACM SIGKDD International Conference on Knowledge Discovery and Data Mining, KDD 2004, pp. 605–610 (2004)
5. Anderka, M., Stein, B., Potthast, M.: Cross-Language High Similarity Search: Why No Sublinear Time Bound Can Be Expected. In: Gurrin, C., He, Y., Kazai, G., Kruschwitz, U., Little, S., Roelleke, T., Rüger, S., van Rijsbergen, K. (eds.) ECIR 2010. LNCS, vol. 5993, pp. 640–644. Springer, Heidelberg (2010)
6. Ture, F., Elsayed, T., Lin, J.J.: No Free Lunch: Brute Force vs. Locality-Sensitive Hashing for Cross-Lingual Pairwise Similarity. In: Proceeding of the 34th International ACM SIGIR Conference on Research and Development in Information Retrieval, SIGIR 2011, pp. 943–952 (2011)
7. Dean, J., Ghemawat, S.: MapReduce: Simplified Data Processing on Large Clusters. Commun. ACM 51(1), 107–113 (2008)
8. Platt, J., Toutanova, K., tau Yih, W.: Translingual Document Representations from Discriminative Projections. In: Proceedings of the 2010 Conference on Empirical Methods in Natural Language Processing. EMNLP 2010, pp. 251–261 (2010)
9. Pouliquen, B., Steinberger, R., Ignat, C.: Automatic Linking of Similar Texts Across Languages. In: Recent Advances in Natural Language Processing III. Selected Papers from RANLP 2003, pp. 307–316 (2003)
10. Steinberger, R., Pouliquen, B., Hagman, J.: Cross-Lingual Document Similarity Calculation Using the Multilingual Thesaurus EUROVOC. In: Gelbukh, A. (ed.) CICLing 2002. LNCS, vol. 2276, pp. 415–424. Springer, Heidelberg (2002)
11. Potthast, M., Stein, B., Anderka, M.: A Wikipedia-Based Multilingual Retrieval Model. In: Macdonald, C., Ounis, I., Plachouras, V., Ruthven, I., White, R.W. (eds.) ECIR 2008. LNCS, vol. 4956, pp. 522–530. Springer, Heidelberg (2008)
12. Brown, P.F., Pietra, V.J.D., Pietra, S.A.D., Mercer, R.L.: The Mathematics of Statistical Machine Translation: Parameter Estimation. Comput. Linguist. 19, 263–311 (1993)
13. Barrón-Cedeño, A., Rosso, P., Pinto, D., Juan, A.: On Cross-lingual Plagiarism Analysis using a Statistical Model. In: Proceedings of the ECAI 2008 Workshop on Uncovering Plagiarism, Authorship and Social Software Misuse, PAN 2008 (2008)
14. Pinto, D., Civera, J., Barrón-Cedeño, A., Juan, A., Rosso, P.: A Statistical Approach to Crosslingual Natural Language Tasks. J. Algorithms 64, 51–60 (2009)
15. Mcnamee, P., Mayfield, J.: Character N-Gram Tokenization for European Language Text Retrieval. Inf. Retr. 7(1-2), 73–97 (2004)
16. Potthast, M., Barrón-Cedeño, A., Stein, B., Rosso, P.: Cross-Language Plagiarism Detection. Language Resources and Evaluation, Special Issue on Plagiarism and Authorship Analysis 45(1) (2011)
17. Pouliquen, B., Steinberger, R., Ignat, C.: Automatic Annotation of Multilingual Text Collections with a Conceptual Thesaurus. CoRR **abs/cs/0609059** (2006)

The Appearance of the Giant Component in Descriptor Graphs and Its Application for Descriptor Selection

Anita Keszler, Levente Kovács, and Tamás Szirányi

Distributed Events Analysis Research Laboratory,
Computer and Automation Research Institute, Hungarian Academy of Sciences,
Kende u. 13-17, Budapest, Hungary
{keszler,levente.kovacs,sziranyi}@sztaki.mta.hu
http://web.eee.sztaki.hu

Abstract. The paper presents a random graph based analysis approach for evaluating descriptors based on pairwise distance distributions on real data. Starting from the Erdős-Rényi model the paper presents results of investigating random geometric graph behaviour in relation with the appearance of the giant component as a basis for choosing descriptors based on their clustering properties. Experimental results prove the existence of the giant component in such graphs, and based on the evaluation of their behaviour the graphs, the corresponding descriptors are compared, and validated in proof-of-concept retrieval tests.

Keywords: feature selection, graph analysis, giant components.

1 Introduction

Content based retrieval in large image/video datasets is highly dependent on the choice of discriminating features and efficient index structures. Recent approaches involve graph based clustering, click searching, and component analysis methods. Open issues remain how to build the graphs (selection of edges and weights), and how to navigate efficiently (neighbourhood search). We propose an approach for feature selection based on the novel investigation of entity difference distributions according to several descriptors and analysing their relation and behaviour w.r.t. graph component formulation and giant component appearances. [1] presents a query by example approach where histograms of point distances are investigated for 2 vs 100 feature dimension for low number of vertices (250), as a basis to show that with increased dimensions the distance distributions tend to be narrower (poor discrimination). Feature selection in the presence of irrelevant features (noise) is introduced in [2]. A method for feature selection [3] is based on an approx. 1000 feature set using heuristics for feature retention, using the sort-merge approach for selecting ranked feature groups. A method for sport video feature selection is presented in [4]; [5] presents a method for automatic image annotation based on a feature weighting scheme and machine learning; [6], [7] present similar approaches for feature selection based on mutual information and principal component analysis. Contrary to other approaches, we do not use artificial feature weighting or a priori clustering, instead we use real data with multiple features and weigh the built graphs by the entities' distances and investigate the behaviour of the distributions and the appearance of the giant component to find descriptors with higher discrimination.

T. Catarci et al. (Eds.): CLEF 2012, LNCS 7488, pp. 76–81, 2012.

2   Giant Components in Geometric Graphs

The appearance of the giant component is a known phenomenon in graph analysis, investigated in several papers, usually for random networks. The results are theoretical thresholds and measurements on the existence of the giant component [8]. Erdős and Rényi (ER) analysed the properties of a random graph with uniformly distributed edges $G(n, p)$ [9] (n is the number of vertices, p is the probability of existence of an edge) which is usually described as a function of parameter c: $p = c/n$. According to Erdős-Rényi, the behaviour of the ER-graph from the point of view of component sizes can be divided into three phases (the size of the largest component is denoted by C_{max}): 1) $c < 1$: $C_{max} = O(\ln n)$ (the graph has small components). 2) $c = 1$: $C_{max} = O(n^{2/3})$; 3) $c > 1$: $C_{max} = O(n)$ (giant component), but all the other components have size $O(\ln n)$.

In random geometric graphs (RGG) the edge-weights are not selected independently [10], thus they are better in mimicking real networks and datasets. The existence of the giant component in RGGs has also been examined. The critical radius of the RGG (with n vertices in d dimensions) is $r_n \sim c \cdot n^{-1/d}$, at which point the average degree in the graph is expected to be constant. Above a certain c threshold there is likely to be a giant component. The exact value of the critical threshold is unknown, only bounds based on simulations are known (e.g. for $d = 2$ see [11]). In our case, this threshold and the value of the RGG radius is very much dependent on the actual feature descriptor, and it is exactly this behaviour that forms the basis of this paper.

2.1   The Appearance of the Giant Component in Real Datasets

The used dataset was collected from television captures in various categories, e.g. sports, nature, cartoons, music, cooking, news, surveillance, etc. The videos were automatically cut into shots (6600 shots, 515 minutes), manually labelled into categories, representative frames extracted. We extracted all the features and the distance of each entity from all the others, enabling the creation of fully connected distance graphs. For evaluating features we selected a set of descriptors: MPEG-7 edge histogram, colour structure, homogeneous texture, colour layout, dominant colour, scalable colour and motion activity [12], average colour, colour segmentation, relative focus regions [13], average motion directions, local binary patterns (LBP) [14], curvelets [15].

The appearance of the giant component in networks with geometric restrictions on the edge weights is an interesting topic on its own. However, it has the potential to be used in applications where the structure of the evolving graph is important as well. E.g. Fig. 1: in (a) and (b) the evolving components are shown depending on the number of graph edges already selected in the graph. In Fig. 1(c), an inner step of the graph building is presented. As we keep selecting the edges by their increasing weights, a giant component will appear, while all the other components stay small. The process ends when all vertices connect to a single component. The descriptor graphs were analysed to trace the appearance of the giant component, and the exact critical threshold can be determined by the analysis of their asymptotic behaviour. Parameters of interest are the size of the largest component compared to the number of vertices and to the 2nd largest component. The critical threshold will be the weight where the ratio of the largest and 2nd largest component sizes decreases below 0.1 and not exceed that threshold later.

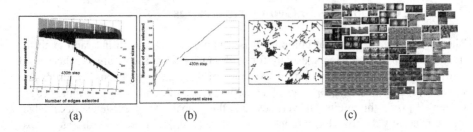

Fig. 1. (a) 3D view of the evolving components in a graph using the edge histogram descriptor. (b) Same diagram top view. (c) Graph at the 430th step and visual excerpt for components during the process (similar entities tend to converge in components which merge at further steps).

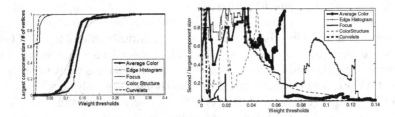

Fig. 2. Left: the largest component in case of different descriptors. Right: ratio of the largest and 2nd largest components for different descriptors.

2.2 Component Parameters, Ranking, Evaluation

In Fig. 2 (left) the ratios of the largest components are compared to the number of vertices at different weight thresholds. The size of the largest component grows rapidly within a small weight range, however, it would be hard to distinguish descriptors based only on this since the evolution of the largest components are similar. Thus we chose the *ratio of the largest and 2nd largest components* as another parameter (Fig. 2 right). While the first parameter shows how fast the largest component grows, the second provides information on how this component suppresses smaller ones. *Critical edge weights* of some of the graphs in Fig. 3 show how critical weights depend on the number of vertices, and the impact of this parameter depends on the descriptor. Detailed test results on the critical weight of the Focus descriptor graph (Fig.3) shows how it depends on the graph size. However, there is a third parameter that should be taken into consideration: the *number of components near the critical threshold* where the giant component suppresses the others (e.g. Fig. 4). The edge histogram-based graph near the critical threshold consists of more components than the one built from the average colour descriptor, which means that before the largest component becomes dominant, the edge histogram descriptor can better divide. This is exactly the property that can serve as the base for automatic selection of better discriminating descriptors.

The above parameters are not always enough to distinguish between descriptors. Our suggestion is to create a fitness function that combines the parameters:

$$F(descr) = w_1 \cdot w_{crit} + w_2 \cdot |C_{sec}| / |C_{max}| + w_3 \cdot N_{comp}/n, \qquad (1)$$

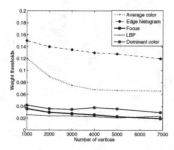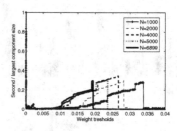

Fig. 3. Left: critical weight values in the graph of different descriptors. Right: ratio of the largest and 2nd largest component sizes of the Focus descriptor graph.

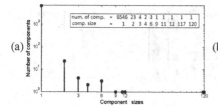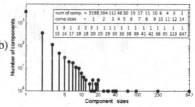

Fig. 4. Component sizes before the critical threshold for different descriptors. (a) Average colour descriptor. (b) Edge histogram descriptor.

where w_{crit} is the graph edge weight where the giant component appears; $|C_{max}|$, $|C_{sec}|$ are the size of the largest and the 2nd largest component, N_{comp} is the number of components at w_{crit}, n is the number of vertices.

First, for each category we took all belonging entities and calculated retrieval precision for all descriptors: $P_{c_i} = max(P_{d_i}(c_i) \cdot wpos_i)$, where $wpos_i$ is the rank weight of d_i descriptor in the specific retrieval run and $P_{d_i}(c_i) = $ (nr of relevant results in c_i using d_i)/(nr of results), 8255 runs in total. The output is summarized in Fig. 5, which shows in (a) for selected c_i categories (horizontal axis) the accumulated ranks of all descriptors (d_i), while Fig. 5(b) shows an example for category c4 how the descriptors take part in producing the results. Then, as a *second step*, we calculated the F values (Eq. 1) for the participating descriptors to also produce a ranking, this time based on graph analysis, taking into consideration the giant component appearances in the descriptor graphs. These results are shown in Fig. 5(c) using weight values of 0.7, 0.2 and 0.1.

Evaluations proved that the graph based process produces a ranking that is close to the exhaustive ground truth ranking, while having important benefits: i). it does not require exhaustive evaluation for all categories and all descriptors in the dataset to produce a ranking, and ii). it is independent of the number of categories and descriptors, providing a ranking based on the discriminating properties of descriptors, without a priori knowledge of dataset internals. The consolidated results of the above evaluations are presented in Fig. 5(d), where 4 queries are used with a fixed result retrieval number of 50 and 100, and using two retrieval approaches: *v1*: results are retrieved without taking into consideration the produced rank, using all available descriptors; *v2*: results

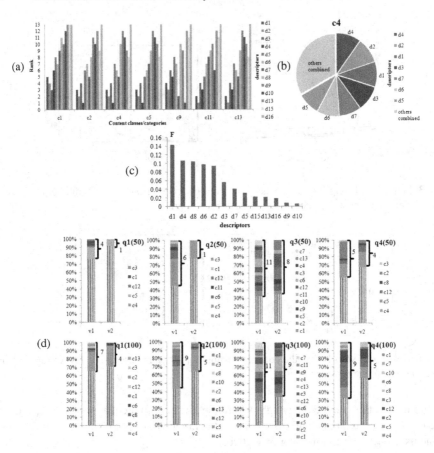

Fig. 5. (a-b) Descriptor ranking evaluation based on their accumulated precision values over classes in the dataset. (a) Ranks of all descriptors (lower is better). (b) An example of how descriptors contribute to retrieval in the case of class c4 (ratios of descriptors' contributions). (c) Descriptor ranks based on the calculated F fitness function values. (d) Retrieval results (precision) for 4 queries (q1-4) for first 50 and first 100 best results (qi(50) and qi(100), $i = \overline{1,4}$). In all graphs $v1$ columns represent retrievals without descriptor ranking, while $v2$ columns represent retrievals where descriptor ranking is taken into consideration. The numbers beside the top of the columns along the curly braces show how irrelevant results are distributed among dataset classes/categories in the specific retrieval process.

are retrieved using the above produced ranking. In this case results are generated using the first 7 best performing descriptors. The figure shows that $v2$ results i). have higher precision, and ii). the returned results contain much lower variation in the number of irrelevant categories. In practice this means that in the case of $v2$ the query responses contain more relevant results and there is less noise in the retrieval.

3   Conclusions and Future Work

We presented results for descriptor selection based on distance graph analysis for the appearance of the giant component. We suggested a fitness function and preformed evaluations to explore the viability of the approach with promising results. Currently the weights of the fitness function need to be set manually and the giant component detection is a standalone process, which needs to be integrated into a retrieval engine itself. We are working to develop a framework for automatic selection of the optimal set of features using the presented approach, and building it into a retrieval engine that can integrate other public video datasets to enable further evaluation.

Acknowledgments. This work was supported by Hungarian Scientific Research Fund (OTKA) grants 83438 and 80352.

References

1. Zhang, W., Men, S., Xu, L., Xu, B.: Feature distribution based quick image retrieval. In: Proc. of Web Information Systems and Applications Conference, pp. 23–28 (2010)
2. Sun, Y., Todorovic, S., Goodison, S.: Local learning based feature selection for high dimensional data analysis. IEEE Trans. on Pattern Analysis and Machine Intelligence 32(9), 1610–1626 (2010)
3. Morris, M., Kender, J.: Sort-merge feature selection and fusion methods for classification of unstructured video. In: Proc. of IEEE International Conference on Multimedia and Expo., pp. 578–581 (2009)
4. Shen, Y., Lu, H., Xue, X.: A Semi-automatic Feature Selecting Method for Sports Video Highlight Annotation. In: Qiu, G., Leung, C., Xue, X.-Y., Laurini, R. (eds.) VISUAL 2007. LNCS, vol. 4781, pp. 38–48. Springer, Heidelberg (2007)
5. Setia, L., Burkhardt, H.: Feature Selection for Automatic Image Annotation. In: Franke, K., Müller, K.-R., Nickolay, B., Schäfer, R. (eds.) DAGM 2006. LNCS, vol. 4174, pp. 294–303. Springer, Heidelberg (2006)
6. Guldogan, E., Gabbouj, M.: Feature selection for content-based image retrieval. Signal, Image and Video Processing 2(3), 241–250 (2008)
7. Li, F., Dai, Q., Xu, W.: Improved similarity-based online feature selection in region-based image retrieval. In: Proc. of IEEE Intl. Conference on Multimedia and Expo., pp. 349–352 (2006)
8. Spenser, J.: The giant component: The golden anniversary. Notices of the AMS 57, 720–724 (1975)
9. Erdős, P., Rényi, A.: On the evolution of random graphs. Publication of the Mathematical Institute of the Hungarian Academy of Sciences (1960)
10. Penrose, M.: Random Geometric Graphs. Oxford University Press (2003)
11. Meester, R., Roy, R.: Continuum Percolation. Cambridge University Press (1996)
12. Manjunath, B.S., Ohm, J.R., Vasudevan, V.V., Yamada, A.: Color and texture descriptors. IEEE Trans. on Circuits and Systems for Video Technology 2(6), 703–715 (2001)
13. Kovács, L., Szirányi, T.: Focus area extraction by blind deconvolution for defining regions of interest. IEEE Tr. on Pattern Analysis and Machine Intelligence 29(6), 1080–1085 (2007)
14. Ojala, T., Pietikainen, M.: Multiresolution gray-scale and rotation invariant texture classification with local binary patterns. IEEE Trans. on Pattern Analysis and Machine Intelligence 24(7) (2002)
15. Candes, E., Demanet, L., Donoho, D., Ying, L.: Fast discrete curvelet transforms. Multiscale Modeling and Simulation 5(3), 861–899 (2006)

Hidden Markov Model
for Term Weighting in Verbose Queries

Xueliang Yan, Guanglai Gao, Xiangdong Su, Hongxi Wei,
Xueliang Zhang, and Qianqian Lu

College of Computer Science,
Inner Mongolia University,
010021 Hohhot, China
{csyxl,csggl,cssxd,cswhx,cszxl,cslqq}@imu.edu.cn

Abstract. It has been observed that short queries generally have better performance than their corresponding long versions when retrieved by the same IR model. This is mainly because most of the current models do not distinguish the importance of different terms in the query. Observed that sentence-like queries encode information related to the term importance in the grammatical structure, we propose a Hidden Markov Model (HMM) based method to extract such information to do term weighting. The basic idea of choosing HMM is motivated by its successful application in capturing the relationship between adjacent terms in NLP field. Since we are dealing with queries of natural language form, we think that HMM can also be used to capture the dependence between the weights and the grammatical structures. Our experiments show that our assumption is quite reasonable and that such information, when utilized properly, can greatly improve retrieval performance.

Keywords: Hidden Markov Model, Verbose Query, Term Weighting.

1 Introduction

Current search engines perform well with keyword queries but are not, in general, effective for verbose queries. This contradicts with our intuition that verbose queries contain more information which can be used to determine the user's information need more accurately. The main reason for this is that most retrieval models treat all the terms in the query as equally important, an assumption that often does not hold, especially for verbose queries.

Many previous works have proposed different methods to deal with the weighting problem and achieved noticeable results. Salton and Buckley [1] incorporate Inverse Document Frequency (IDF) into Vector Space Model (VSM), which can be regarded as the earliest weighting scheme. Kumaran and Allan [2] address this problem by detecting the best sub-query by the Kruskal's minimum spanning tree algorithm and show that rewriting the query to a version that comprises a small subset of appropriate terms from the original query greatly improves effectiveness. Later, Kumaran and Allan [3] propose another sub-query detection method which incorporates user interaction into consideration. Recently,

T. Catarci et al. (Eds.): CLEF 2012, LNCS 7488, pp. 82–87, 2012.
© Springer-Verlag Berlin Heidelberg 2012

machine learning techniques are gradually adopted to deal with this problem. Bendersky and Croft [4] develop a technique for automatic extraction of key concepts from verbose queries and propose a probabilistic model for integrating the weighted key concepts into a query. Observed that the quality of the returned terms from Pseudo Relevance Feedback (PRF) methods are mostly not useful for expansion, Cao et al. [5] propose to use C-SVM to distinguish good expansion terms from bad ones for PRF. In this case, they are distinguishing weights, Good or Bad, for expanded terms.

In spite of the successfulness of previous works, we find that none of them have considered the grammatical structure related information embedded in the sentence-like queries. We believe that there must be some underlying weighting consideration related to the structure when people formulating a natural language sentence, consciously or non-consciously. In this paper, we propose a Hidden Markov Model (HMM) [6] based method to capture such relationships between the structure and weights. The idea of choosing HMM is motivated by its successful application in capturing the relationship between adjacent terms in NLP field (such as part-of-speech tagging) and the fact that we are dealing with queries of natural language form. Our basic idea is that since the HMM can tag the terms with their part-of-speeches, it can similarly tag the terms with labels indicating their relative importance given appropriate linguistic features. We conduct our experiments on the standard TREC test collection. Experimental results show that our idea is feasible.

The rest of the paper is organized as follows: Section 2 describes our Hidden Markov Model based weighting method. In Section 3, we present a series of experiments on the TREC standard collection. Finally, conclusions and future work are outlined in Section 4.

2   Hidden Markov Model for Term Weighting

Hidden Markov Model (HMM) is one model of the statistical model families. The HMM has a sequence of hidden states each has an observation associated with it. Since we can not see the states directly, we have to estimate them from the observations exposed to us [6]. In our case, we will take the grammatical features as the observation and the weight levels of the query terms as the hidden states. We can then consider the weight level sequence as a Markov Random Process as shown in Fig. 1. All we need to do is finding the weight level sequence that has the highest probability of generating the observed feature sequence. Formally, we want to find the weight level sequence WLS^* that satisfies (1):

$$WLS^* = \underset{WLS}{\arg\max} P\left(WLS|FS\right) . \tag{1}$$

Applying some probability algebra, we can easily get (2):

$$WLS^* = \underset{WLS}{\arg\max} \left[\prod_{i=1}^{m} P\left(WLS_i|WLS_{i-1}\right) * P\left(FS_i|WLS_i\right) \right] . \tag{2}$$

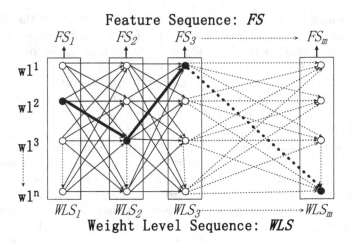

Fig. 1. The HMM for the feature sequence *FS* and weight level sequence *WLS*, where FS_i denotes the observed feature for the ith term and WLS_i denotes the weight level of term i which may take value from the possible weight level set $\{wl^1, wl^2, \ldots, wl^n\}$. Observed the feature sequence *FS*, we want to determine the most probable weight level sequence WLS^*, like the one represented by the solid nodes.

Then we can solve (2) efficiently by applying the Viterbi algorithm [6].

In this work, we will adopt our method to the language modeling framework proposed by Metzler and Croft [7] which incorporates weighting parameters as shown in (3):

$$\log p\left(Q|D\right) = \sum_{i=1}^{m} w_i \log p\left(Q_i|D\right) \ . \tag{3}$$

In their framework, the specific method for the estimation of weighting parameters $\{w_1, w_2, \ldots, w_m\}$ are not assumed. Then our work is to estimate them for sentence-like queries based on the HMM model.

3   Experiments

To test our idea, we implement our model on the specific linguistic feature, part-of-speech (POS), i.e., the features in (2) are now instanced by the POSs of the terms. We choose POS of the terms as the feature because intuition tells us that POS usually has a strong relationship with the importance of a term. For example, *noun* usually indicates that a term is important. However, there are other things to consider, for example: are all *nouns* of the same importance? If not, do any statistical weighting dependencies exist between the POSs in the sentence patterns? Intuition tells us that it does. For example, for combination type of NN+IN+NN ("use of land", "application of spaceborne", "type of product", etc.), we generally believe that the second *nouns* are more important than the first ones. According to our statistics, the first NN is much less important

Table 1. Experimental results. *BL* means baseline. Scores with * and + mean significantly better than their corresponding baselines with $p < 0.05$ and $p < 0.01$ respectively.

	BL	TopicSet_1		TopicSet_2		TopicSet_3		TopicSet_4		TopicSet_5	
		MAP	*P@5*	*MAP*	*P@5*	*MAP*	*P@5*	*MAP*	*P@5*	*MAP*	*P@5*
QL		0.184	0.348	0.157	0.400	0.215	0.436	0.326	0.567	0.279	0.500
TS	QL	0.236^+_*	0.448^+_*	0.206^+_*	0.527^+_*	0.256^+_*	0.492^+_*	0.361^+_*	0.608^+_*	0.305^+_*	0.538^+_*
OKAPI		0.188	0.348	0.165	0.425	0.221	0.432	0.321	0.551	0.279	0.508
KC		0.212	0.356	0.196	0.468	0.226	0.440	0.343	0.552	0.308	0.571
HMM	KC	0.213	0.368	0.189	0.468	0.224	0.444	0.335	0.564	0.291	0.514
K+H	KC	0.219	0.368	0.202	0.476	0.230	0.448	0.350	0.576	0.309	0.563

than the second one most of the time. Other combinations also have similar phenomenon. Now, we want to test if our HMM model can capture such relationships automatically and in turn improve the overall retrieval performance.

3.1 Experimental Setting

We conduct our experiments on the data set for TREC Robust04 track which consists of 250 topics (Topics 301-450 and Topics 601-700) and 528155 documents. We choose Robust04 since the descriptive parts of its topics are mostly verbose sentences which fulfill the requirement of adopting our model. The part-of-speech tagger we adopted is an implementation of the log-linear part-of-speech taggers [8], which can be downloaded from its author's website.[1] The tagger uses the Penn Treebank Tagset[2] which has a total of 45 different tags. We use the Indri Search Engine [9] in the Lemur Toolkit[3] to perform retrieval. The training of HMM needs a training set. Since we didn't find a public one with weights annotated, we manually construct one by assigning each term in the 250 topics with a 6-leveled weighting value. Five-fold cross validation is performed to test the performance since the data for testing should be different from that for training.

3.2 Experimental Results

The experimental results are summarized in Tab. 1.

Since the weights labeled in the training set are very subjective, we first test its suitableness for training. Here, we take the Query Likelihood (QL) method as the baseline, i.e., assigning weight parameters in (3) with the same value. In Tab. 1, we can see that the performance achieved by the training set (TS) can greatly outperform that achieved by the QL method which does not consider term importance at all. This indicates that if the learning process is effective, the retrieval performance of the testing runs will also be greatly improved.

---

[1] http://nlp.stanford.edu/software/tagger.shtml
[2] http://www.computing.dcu.ie/~acahill/tagset.html
[3] http://www.lemurproject.org

In Tab. 1, we also list the results achieved by our HMM based method to-gether with the ones by some other methods for comparison. More specifically, OKAPI denotes the Okapi BM25 [10] method implemented in Indri with default parameters ($k1 : 1.2$, $b : 0.75$, $k3 : 7$) [9]; KC denotes the Key Concept method in [4]. We can observe that the HMM perform better than both the QL and OKAPI methods which assume equal weighting assumption. This shows that our HMM based approach can really capture the relative importance of the terms. We can also observe that the results achieved by the KC method and that by our HMM method are close to each other. This indicates that the amount of weighting information embedded in the organization of POS is comparable to that KC method has used.

We have mentioned that we are using a different type of information to address the term weighting problem. This means that there is potential to combine our method with other works. Here, we do some initial tests at the result level and show that this combination is possible. To do this, we first generate the ranked document lists by the two methods independently. After normalizing the score for each document d to the same scale (0–1), we re-rank the documents according to equation (4) [11]:

$$score_{K+H}(d) = w_{KC} * norm\_score_{KC}(d) + w_{HMM} * norm\_score_{HMM}(d) ,\quad (4)$$

where w_{KC} and w_{HMM} are the combination parameters whose ratio is $1 : 0.46$ and are set empirically. From Tab. 1, we can observe that the performance of the combined method K+H (combination of KC and HMM) is a little better than both the HMM and the KC method alone, although not very significant, but at least consistent on all the 5-folds. So we still have reason to believe the potential of combining the two methods to achieve better performance.

4 Conclusions

In this paper, we have proposed a novel query term weighting scheme that can capture the weighting information in the structure of queries with natural lan-guage form. Our basic idea is that, for queries of this type, the weight gen-eration process can be viewed as a Markov Random Process and that it can be estimated by the observable grammatical feature sequence. Experimental re-sults show that we get similar performance when compared to the Key Concept weighting method. One question might be proposed is that why we should be interested in this HMM scheme since it can not greatly outperform the previous KC method. The key point is that the information adopted by our method is totally different from that used by others. It's more reasonable to compare with other methods that using the same information. However, by far, no previous work has used this type of information. On the other hand, this means that there is potential to combine our method with others, i.e., to combine different kinds of information to make the weights more accurate. To test this assumption, we did some initial combination experiments and achieved results with expected im-provement. One point should be noted is about the combination method. In our experiments we just perform the linear combinations of HMM with KC at result level. To further improve retrieval performance, we think it would be more rational to combine the two methods at earlier training stage instead of at the result level where individual decisions have been made. What's more, we should adopt different combination parameters for different queries, not all being the fixed one (1:0.46 in our case). Another point is that we have implemented our model on the POS sequence. Other features may achieve better performance, like the tree structure of a natural language sentence. But this may require other models instead of HMM. We plan to test all these ideas for future study.

Acknowledgments. We would like to thank Prof. Jian-Yun Nie of Université de Montréal for his invaluable suggestions.

References

1. Salton, G., Buckley, C.: Term-Weighting Approaches in Automatic Text Retrieval. Information Processing and Management 24(5), 513–523 (1988)
2. Kumaran, G., Allan, J.: A Case for Shorter Queries and Helping Users Create Them. In: Human Language Technology Conference of the North American Chapter of the Association of Computational Linguistics, Rochester, pp. 220–227 (2007)
3. Kumaran, G., Allan, J.: Effective and Efficient User Interaction for Long Queries. In: 31st Annual International ACM SIGIR Conference on Research and Development in Information Retrieval, pp. 11–18. ACM Press, Singapore (2008)
4. Bendersky, M., Croft, W.B.: Discovering Key Concepts in Verbose Queries. In: 31st Annual International ACM SIGIR Conference on Research and Development in Information Retrieval, pp. 491–498. ACM Press, Singapore (2008)
5. Cao, G., Nie, J., Gao, J., Robertson, S.: Selecting Good Expansion Terms for Pseudo-Relevance Feedback. In: 31st Annual International ACM SIGIR Conference on Research and Development in Information Retrieval, pp. 243–250. ACM Press, Singapore (2008)
6. Rabiner, L.R.: A Tutorial on Hidden Markov Models and Selected Applications in Speech Recognition. Proceedings of the IEEE 77(2), 257–286 (1989)
7. Metzler, D., Croft, W.B.: Combining the Language Model and Inference Network Approaches to Retrieval. Information Processing and Management 40(5), 735–750 (2004)
8. Toutanova, K., Klein, D., Manning, C.D., Singer, Y.: Feature-Rich Part-of-Speech Tagging with a Cyclic Dependency Network. In: Human Language Technology Conference of the North American Chapter of the Association for Computational Linguistics, Edmonton, pp. 252–259 (2003)
9. Metzler, D., Strohman, T., Zhou, Y., Croft, W.B.: Indri at TREC 2005: Terabyte Track. In: 14th Text Retrieval Conference, Gaithersburg, pp. 175–180 (2005)
10. Jones, K.S., Walker, S., Robertson, S.E.: A Probabilistic Model of Information Retrieval: Development and Comparative Experiments. Information Processing and Management 36(6), 779–840 (2000)
11. Croft, W.B.: Combining Approaches to Information Retrieval. In: Croft, W.B. (ed.) Advances in Information Retrieval: Recent Research from the Center for Intelligent Information Retrieval, pp. 1–36. Kluwer Academic Publishers (2000)

DIRECTions: Design and Specification of an IR Evaluation Infrastructure

Maristella Agosti, Emanuele Di Buccio, Nicola Ferro, Ivano Masiero,
Simone Peruzzo, and Gianmaria Silvello

Department of Information Engineering, University of Padua, Italy
{agosti,dibuccio,ferro,masieroi,peruzzos,silvello}@dei.unipd.it

Abstract. *Information Retrieval (IR)* experimental evaluation is an essential part of the research on and development of information access methods and tools. Shared data sets and evaluation scenarios allow for comparing methods and systems, understanding their behaviour, and tracking performances and progress over the time. On the other hand, experimental evaluation is an expensive activity in terms of human effort, time, and costs required to carry it out.

Software and hardware infrastructures that support experimental evaluation operation as well as management, enrichment, and exploitation of the produced scientific data provide a key contribution in reducing such effort and costs and carrying out systematic and throughout analysis and comparison of systems and methods, overall acting as enablers of scientific and technical advancement in the field. This paper describes the specification for an IR evaluation infrastructure by conceptually modeling the entities involved in IR experimental evaluation and their relationships and by defining the architecture of the proposed evaluation infrastructure and the APIs for accessing it.

1 Motivations

IR has always been a scientific field strongly rooted in experimentation and collaborative evaluation efforts [1]. Large-scale evaluation initiatives, such as TREC in the United States[1], the CLEF in Europe[2], and the NTCIR in Asia[3], contribute significantly to advancements in research and industrial innovation in the IR field, and to the building of strong research communities. Beside their scientific and industrial impact, a recent study conducted by NIST highlighted also the economic impact and value of large-scale evaluation campaigns and reported that for every \$1 that NIST and its partners invested in TREC, at least \$3.35 to \$5.07 in benefits accrued to IR researchers and developers while the overall investment in TREC has been estimated in about 30 million dollars [2].

IR evaluation is challenged by variety and fragmentation in many respects – diverse tasks and metrics, heterogeneous collections, different systems, and alternative approaches for managing the experimental data. Not only does this

---

[1] http://trec.nist.gov/
[2] http://www.clef-initiative.eu/
[3] http://research.nii.ac.jp/ntcir/index-en.html

T. Catarci et al. (Eds.): CLEF 2012, LNCS 7488, pp. 88–99, 2012.

hamper the generalizability and exploitability of the results but it also increases the effort and costs needed to produce such experimental results and to further exploit them. Abstracting over these constituents as well as over the obtained results is crucial for scaling-up evaluation and evaluation infrastructures are a fundamental part of this wider abstraction process [3].

When it comes to analysis of the experimental results, several methodologies, metrics, and statistical techniques have been proposed over the years [4]. Nevertheless, it is often difficult to apply them properly, sometimes due to their complexity and the required competencies, and in a way that eases further comparison and interpretations, e.g. by choosing similar values for parameters or equivalent normalization and transformation strategies for the data. An evaluation infrastructure should not only facilitate this day-to-day analyses but it should also be able to preserve and provide access over time to them in order to support and foster the conduction and automation of longitudinal studies which track the evolution of the performances over the time, as for example [5].

An important, but often overlooked, part of analysis is the visualization of the experimental data. Visualization in IR has been mostly applied to alternative presentation of search results [6,7] while, when applied to the experimental data, it can greatly impact their comprehension and understanding, as it has been done in [8,9]. Not only visualization but also visual interaction with the experimental data and analytical models supporting such interaction, as those developed in the *Visual Analytics (VA)* field [10], should be exploited in order to facilitate the exploration and study of the experimental data. This latter possibility, i.e. VA for IR evaluation, becomes feasible only when there is an evaluation infrastructure supporting and implementing such analytical and interaction models and it has been started to be studied only very recently [11,12].

This paper presents the specification of the evaluation infrastructure which is being developed in the context of the PROMISE project[4], an European network of excellence which aims at improving the access to the scientific data produced during evaluation activities, supporting the organization and running of evaluation campaigns, increasing automation in the evaluation process, and fostering the usage of the managed scientific data. Three key contributions are discussed: (i) the conceptual schema which describes the entities involved in the experimental evaluation and the relationships among them; (ii) the architecture of the evaluation infrastructure able to manage scientific data; (iii) a set of Web API to interact with all the resources managed by the system.

The presentation is organized as follows: Section 2 reports on previous works; Section 3 describes the results of the conceptual modeling; Section 4 gives an overview of the architecture; and Section 5 presents a use case scenario based on the visualization of topics, experiments, and metrics; finally, Section 6 draws some final remarks.

---

[4] http://www.promise-noe.eu/

2   Background

During their life-span, large-scale evaluation campaigns produce valuable amounts of scientific data which are the basis for the subsequent scientific work and system development, thus constituting an essential reference for the field. Until a few years ago, limited attention had been paid to the modeling, management, curation, and access of the produced scientific data, even though the importance of scientific data in general has been highlighted by many different institutional organizations, such as the European Commission [13].

The research group on Information Management Systems of the Department of Information Engineering of the University of Padua[5] started a few years ago the challenge of addressing the most common limitations on facing the issue [14] and working on envisaging and defining a necessary infrastructure for dealing with the complexity of the challenge. We have proposed an extension to the traditional evaluation methodology in order to explicitly take into consideration and model the valuable scientific data produced during an evaluation campaign, the creation of which is often expensive and not easily reproducible. Indeed, researchers not only benefit from having comparable experiments and a reliable assessment of their performances, but they also take advantage of the possibility of having an integrated vision of the scientific data produced, together with their analyses and interpretations, as well as benefiting from the possibility of keeping, re-using, preserving, and curating them. Moreover, the way in which experimental results are managed is an integral part of the process of knowledge transfer and sharing towards relevant application communities, which needs to properly understand these experimental results in order to create and assess their own systems. Therefore, we have undertaken the design of an evaluation infrastructure for large-scale evaluation campaigns and the outcome is the *Distributed Information Retrieval Evaluation Campaign Tool (DIRECT)*, which manages the scientific data produced during a large-scale evaluation campaign, as well as supports the archiving, access, citation, dissemination, and sharing of the experimental results [15,16].

In the context of the international DESIRE workshop [17], the necessity for open and public benchmarks and infrastructures has been confirmed as they represent the foundations of the scientific method adopted in the IR community. Algorithms and solutions tested and evaluated on private data not publicly accessible make it difficult for researchers and developers to reproduce them, verify their performances, and compare them with the state-of-the-art or with own solutions. Another important point that has been highlighted is the need for a proper and shared modeling of the experimental data produced by IR evaluation, in terms of conceptual model, descriptive metadata, and their semantic enrichment.

The effort reported in this paper represents an evolution of DIRECT in line with the feedback received over the years and discussions raised by experts during the DESIRE workshop, since our final goal is to deliver a unified infrastructure

---

[5] http://www.dei.unipd.it/wdyn/?IDsezione=3314&IDgruppo_pass=121

and environment for data, knowledge, tools, methodologies and the user community in order to advance the experimental evaluation of complex multimedia and multilingual information systems.

3   Conceptual Modeling of the Evaluation Infrastructure

A conceptual schema provides the means for modeling and representing the reality of interest, lays the foundations for the automatic processing and managing of the identified entities, and it is one of the steps of that abstraction process needed in IR evaluation, as discussed in Section 1. In the context of IR evaluation this is particularly important for reducing the human effort required by evaluation activities and to move experimental evaluation from a handicraft process towards a more "industrial" one. Finally, a conceptual schema provides the basis for managing, making accessible, preserving and enriching experimental data over time. This is especially relevant in the IR field since not only are the experimental data the basis for all the subsequent research and scientific production, but they are also extremely valuable from an economic point of view, as discussed in Section 1.

The conceptual schema of the infrastructure is organised into eight functional areas; Figure 1 provides an intuitive representation of them. The remainder of this section provides a brief description of these areas.

Resource Management area: This area supports the interaction between users/groups and the resources handled by the infrastructure. Resources can be actual data adopted in or produced by evaluation activities, e.g. experimental collections or experiment results, as well as the evaluation activities and tasks carried out within them. With the term *resource* we refer to a generic entity that concerns evaluation activities and with which a user or a group of users can interact.

Metadata area: This area supports the description and the enrichment through metadata of the resources handled by the infrastructure.

Evaluation Activity area: This area identifies the core of the infrastructure; it refers to activities aimed at evaluating applications, systems, and methodologies for multimodal and multimedia information access and retrieval. Entities in this area are not limited to traditional evaluation campaigns, but they also include trial and education activities. *Trial* refers to an evaluation activity that may be actively run by, say, a research group, a person or a corporate body for their own interest. This evaluation activity may be or may not be shared with the community of interest; for instance, a trial activity may be the experiments performed to write a research paper or the activities conducted to evaluate a Web application. The *Education* activities allow us to envision evaluation activities carried out for educational purposes.

Experimental Collection area: This area allows us to set up a traditional IR evaluation environment and to manage the different collections made available by the diverse evaluation forums. A classical IR experimental collection

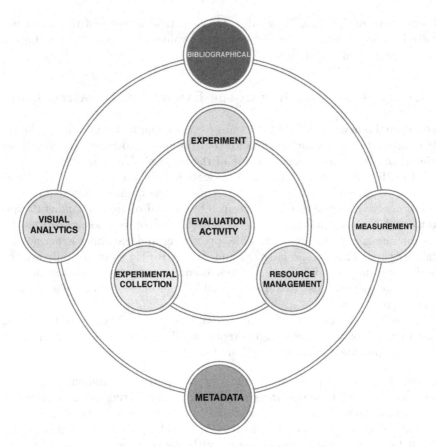

Fig. 1. The conceptual areas of the Evaluation Infrastructure

is a triple composed by a corpus of documents, a group of topics and a set of assessments on the documents with regard to the considered topics. In the abstraction process particular attention has been paid to the the concept of *topic*, because of the diversity of the information needs that have to be addressed in different evaluation tasks.

Experiment area: This area concerns the scientific data produced by an experiment carried out during an evaluation activity. The evaluation infrastructure considers three different types of experiment: run, guerrilla, and living. A *Run* is defined as a ranked list of documents for each topic in the experimental collection [18]. A *Guerrilla* experiment identifies an evaluation activity performed on corporate IR systems (e.g. a custom search engine integrated in a corporate Web site). A *Living* experiment deals with the specific experimental data resulting from the Living Retrieval Laboratories, which will examine the use of operational systems as experimental platform on which to conduct user-based experiments to scale.

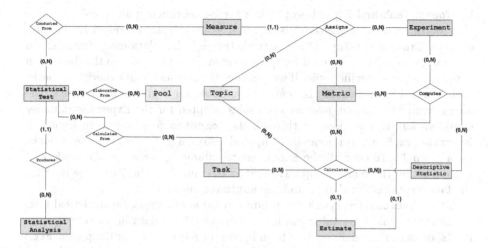

Fig. 2. The ER Schema modeling the Measurement Area

Bibliographical area: This area is responsible for making explicit and re-
taining the relationship between the data that result from the evaluation
activities and the scientific production based on these data.
Measurement area: This area concerns the measures used for evaluation
activities.
Visual Analytics area: This area manages the information used by the infrastructure to store and recover whichever visualization of the data that the
users do.

In the remainder we will focus on the measurement and visual analytics areas
because they provide concrete cases for some of the issues discussed in Section 1.

3.1   Measurement Area

The Measurement area concerns the measures adopted for evaluation activities.
Figure 2 shows the ER schema of this area; Metric is the main entity and it
refers to a standard of measurement allowing us to quantify the effectiveness
and the efficiency of a system under evaluation and also to optimize systems
themselves. The Measure entity represents the value of a Metric calculated
on some experiments handled by the infrastructure. Other entities in this area
are: Statistical Analysis which represents a list of the statistical analyses
supported by the infrastructure, Descriptive statistics which are used to
describe the basic features of the data in a study, and Statistical test which
provides a mechanism for making quantitative decisions about a process or processes. The estimated numerical value of a Descriptive Statistic calculated
by the infrastructure is represented by the Estimate entity.

Figure 2 depicts the relationships among these entities and other entities in
the evaluation activity, the experimental collection, and the experiment area,

i.e. `Topic`, `Task` and `Experiment`. For a topic-experiment pair a specific value of a metric, namely a measure, is assigned – i.e. a `Measure` refers to one and only one `Experiment-Topic-Metric` triple through the relationship `Assigns`; an example is the value computed for the metric average precision on the data of an experiment for a specific topic. If we consider the results on an experiment basis, then `Descriptive Statistics` can be computed for a given `Metric` – e.g. the Mean Average Precision over all the topics adopted for the `Experiment` under consideration; this is modeled through the `Computes` relationship in Figure 2. `Descriptive Statistics` can be computed also on a task basis, e.g. the variance for a given `Topic` over all the `Experiments` submitted for a specific `Task`; this is modeled by the relationship `Calculates` that involves the `Task`, the `Metric`, the `Descriptive Statistic` and the `Estimate` entities.

A `Statistical Analysis` can produce a value for a specific statistical test; the `Statistical Test` value can be `Elaborated From` data in no, one or more `Pools`, or `Calculated From` data from no, one or more `Tasks`, or `Computed From` an `Experiment`. Lastly, a `Statistical Test` value can be obtained by the test `Conducted` on no, one or more `Measures`.

The main point here is that explicitly considering the entities in the measurement area as a part of the conceptual schema we are able to retain and make accessible not only experimental data, but also evaluation methodologies and the context wherein metrics and methodologies have been applied. It is our opinion that this is crucial for the definition and the adoption of shared evaluation protocols, which is the main aim of international evaluation initiatives.

3.2   Visual Analytics Area

The Visual Analytics area manages the information used by the infrastructure to store and retrieve parametric and interactive visualization of the data. Indeed, visualizations are not static objects but dynamic ones which are built up via subsequent interactions of the users with the experimental data and the infrastructure. The main entities are: `Visualization` which refers to the information used by the infrastructure to store a visualization of the data as well as the history of all the interactions of a user with the experimental data, and `Snapshot` which stores the snapshots of a given visualization. The relationships among the entities in this area are depicted in Figure 3.

Figure 3 also depicts the relationship between the `Visualization` entity and entities in the Evaluation Activity, the Experimental Collection, the Experiment and the Measurement area. Every visualization can be related to no, one or more `Tasks` – see relationship `ViTa`, to no, one or more `Pools` – see relationship `ViPo`, to no, one or more `Experiments` – see relationship `ViEx`, to no, one or more `Statistical Tests` – and see relationship `ViSt`.

4   Architecture of the Evaluation Infrastructure

The architecture of the evaluation infrastructure is based on the introduced conceptual model and stems from an evolution of the DIRECT [16] system.

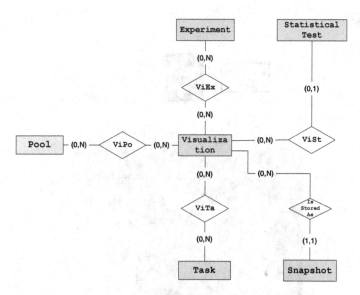

Fig. 3. The relationships between the **Visualization** entity and entities in the Evaluation Activity, the Experimental Collection, the Experiment and the Measurement area

The architecture and the implementation of the system have been developed by exploiting open source technologies, software and frameworks, in order to guarantee a platform which is cooperative, modular, scalable, sustainable over time and allowing interoperability among different systems.

Figure 4 shows the architecture of the system. The right stack summarizes the layers modeling the application, while the left stack shows the building blocks of the implementation of the system. At the lowest levels of the stack – see point (1) of Figure 4 – data stored into database and indexes are mapped to resources and vice versa. The communication with the upper levels is granted through the mechanism of the *Data Access Object (DAO)* pattern. The application logic layer is in charge of the high-level tasks made by the system, such as the enrichment of raw data, the calculation of metrics and the carrying out of statistical analyses on experiments. These resources, shown at point (2), are therefore accessible by remote devices via HTTP through a *REpresentational State Transfer (REST)*ful Web service, represented by points (3) and (5).

The Access Control Infrastructure, point (4), takes care of monitoring the various resources and functionalities offered by the system. It performs authentication by asking for user credentials to log it into the system, and authorization by verifying if the logged in user requesting an operation holds sufficient rights to perform it. The logging infrastructure, which lays behind all the components of the DIRECT system, captures information such as the user name, the *Internet Protocol (IP)* address of the connecting host, the action invoked by the user, the messages exchanged among the components of the system, and any

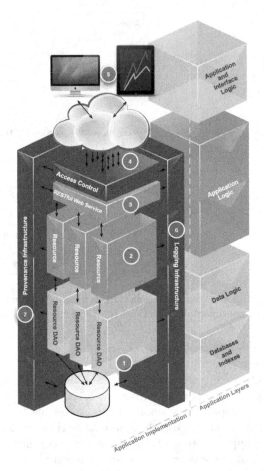

Fig. 4. The Architecture of the DIRECT System as a REST Web Service

error condition, if necessary. The Provenance Infrastructure – point (7) in Figure 4 – is in charge of keeping track of the full lineage of each resource managed by the system since its first creation, allowing granted users to reconstruct its full history and modifications over time.

Next section will focus on the RESTful Web Service level (3) and reports on a use case scenario for accessing experimental data when considering the inter-area involving topics, experiments and metrics.

5 Use Case Scenario: Tasks, Experiments, and Metrics

This use case scenario describes how the users of the DIRECT system can access experimental data about task, experiments, and related metrics in order to process them.

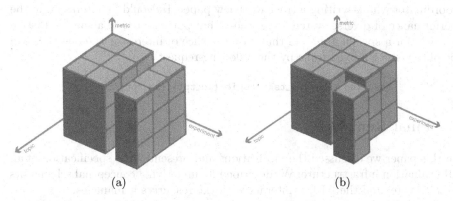

Fig. 5. Topics, Experiments, and Metrics Data Matrix Sliced on a fixed Experiment (Figure 5a), and for a fixed Topic-Experiment pair (Figure 5b).

An HTTP GET request for a task with identifier `id_tsk` and namespace `ns_tsk`:

$$\texttt{/task/\{id\_tsk\};\{ns\_tsk\}/metric}$$

will provide data about topics, experiments, and metrics as response, which can be thought of as the three-dimensional matrix, or *Online Analytical Processing (OLAP)* data cubes [19], as those sketched in Figure 5.

The data cube can be rotated (pivot operation) to show topics, experiments and metrics as rows or columns, providing alternative visualizations of data that the user can save and export as snapshots. It is also possible to select and reorder rows or columns, and slice portions of cube, as shown in Figure 5.

Let us consider the case of a user that is interested in an experiment, specifically how an approach performs on each single topic when considering all the distinct metrics made available by the infrastructure. Figure 5a shows the slice of the OLAP Data Cube that can interest this user. The HTTP GET request provided to the DIRECT system to gather all the data about an experiment will be: the URL `http://direct.dei.unipd.it/` followed by

$$\texttt{task/\{id\_tsk\};\{ns\_tsk\}/experiment/\{id\_exp\};\{ns\_exp\}/metric}$$

For each slice it is possible to refine the request specifying two parameters instead of one, then obtaining a single column from the sliced data cube. For example, if the user is interested in the system performance on a specific topic, the HTTP GET request will be:

$$\texttt{task/\{id\_tsk\};\{ns\_tsk\}/topic/\{id\_tpt\};\{ns\_tpc\}}$$

$$\texttt{/experiment/\{id\_exp\};\{ns\_exp\}/metric}$$

The response of this request corresponds to a single column of the data cube that provides information for all the metrics for a given topic in the context of a given experiment – see Figure 5b. Another example could involve a track coordinator who is writing a track overview paper. He could be interested in the performance of diverse systems, e.g. those that participated to a specific task in a track, for a specific topic; in that case the slice of interest is the one that can be obtained for a fixed topic by the following request

$$\texttt{task/\{id\_tsk\};\{ns\_tsk\}/topic/\{id\_tpt\};\{ns\_tpt\}/metric}$$

6   Final Remarks

In this paper we discussed the motivations and presented the specification of an IR evaluation infrastructure. We described its underlying conceptual schema, its architecture, and the API to interact with the resources it manages.

Besides supporting the design of an innovative evaluation infrastructure, another goal of this work is to propose a common abstraction of IR evaluation activities that can be exploited to: (i) share and re-use the valuable scientific data produced by experiments and analysis, (ii) employ innovative and interactive visual analytics techniques in IR experimental evaluation, and (iii) envision evaluation activities other than traditional IR campaigns.

Acknowledgements. The authors wish to thanks Marco Dussin for his contributions to the definition of the infrastructure to which he has contributed while he was part of the team of the University of Padua. The authors wish to thanks all PROMISE partners for the useful discussions on many aspects related to the evaluation infrastructure.

The work reported in this paper has been supported by the PROMISE network of excellence (contract n. 258191) project as a part of the 7th Framework Program of the European commission (FP7/2007-2013).

References

1. Harman, D.K.: Information Retrieval Evaluation. Morgan & Claypool Publishers, USA (2011)
2. Rowe, B.R., Wood, D.W., Link, A.L., Simoni, D.A.: Economic Impact Assessment of NIST's Text REtrieval Conference (TREC) Program. RTI Project Number 0211875, RTI International, USA (2010),
   http://trec.nist.gov/pubs/2010.economic.impact.pdf
3. Allan, J., et al.: Frontiers, Challenges, and Opportunities for Information Retrieval – Report from SWIRL 2012. In: The Second Strategic Workshop on Information Retrieval in Lorne, SIGIR Forum, vol. 46 (in print, February 2012)
4. Sanderson, M.: Test Collection Based Evaluation of Information Retrieval Systems. Foundations and Trends in Information Retrieval (FnTIR) 4, 247–375 (2010)
5. Armstrong, T.G., Moffat, A., Webber, W., Zobel, J.: Improvements That Don't Add Up: Ad-Hoc Retrieval Results Since 1998. In: Proc. 18th International Conference on Information and Knowledge Management (CIKM 2009), pp. 601–610. ACM Press, New York (2009)
6. Zhang, J.: Visualization for Information Retrieval. Springer, Heidelberg (2008)

7. Newman, D., Baldwin, T., Cavedon, L., Huang, E., Karimi, S., Martínez, D., Scholer, F., Zobel, J.: Visualizing Search Results and Document Collections Using Topic Maps. Journal of Web Semantics 8, 169–175 (2010)

8. Banks, D., Over, P., Zhang, N.F.: Blind Men and Elephants: Six Approaches to TREC data. Information Retrieval 1, 7–34 (1999)

9. Sormunen, E., Hokkanen, S., Kangaslampi, P., Pyy, P., Sepponen, B.: Query performance analyser: a web-based tool for ir research and instruction. In: Järvelin, K., Beaulieu, M., Baeza-Yates, R., Hyon Myaeng, S. (eds.) Proceedings of SIGIR 2002, p. 450. ACM, New York (2002)

10. Keim, D.A., Mansmann, F., Schneidewind, J., Ziegler, H.: Challenges in Visual Data Analysis. In: Banissi, E. (ed.) Proc. of the 10th International Conference on Information Visualization (IV 2006), pp. 9–16. IEEE Computer Society, Los Alamitos (2006)

11. Di Buccio, E., Dussin, M., Ferro, N., Masiero, I., Santucci, G., Tino, G.: To Rerank or to Re-query: Can Visual Analytics Solve This Dilemma? In: Forner, P., Gonzalo, J., Kekäläinen, J., Lalmas, M., de Rijke, M. (eds.) CLEF 2011. LNCS, vol. 6941, pp. 119–130. Springer, Heidelberg (2011)

12. Ferro, N., Sabetta, A., Santucci, G., Tino, G.: Visual Comparison of Ranked Result Cumulated Gains. In: Miksch, S., Santucci, G. (eds.) Proc. 2nd International Workshop on Visual Analytics (EuroVA 2011), pp. 21–24. Eurographics Association, Goslar (2011)

13. European Union: Riding the wave. How Europe can gain from the rising tide of scientific data. Printed by Osmotica.it, Final report of the High level Expert Group on Scientific Data (2010)

14. Agosti, M., Di Nunzio, G.M., Ferro, N.: Scientific Data of an Evaluation Campaign: Do We Properly Deal with Them? In: Peters, C., Clough, P., Gey, F.C., Karlgren, J., Magnini, B., Oard, D.W., de Rijke, M., Stempfhuber, M. (eds.) CLEF 2006. LNCS, vol. 4730, pp. 11–20. Springer, Heidelberg (2007)

15. Di Nunzio, G.M., Ferro, N.: DIRECT: A System for Evaluating Information Access Components of Digital Libraries. In: Rauber, A., Christodoulakis, S., Tjoa, A.M. (eds.) ECDL 2005. LNCS, vol. 3652, pp. 483–484. Springer, Heidelberg (2005)

16. Dussin, M., Ferro, N.: Managing the Knowledge Creation Process of Large-Scale Evaluation Campaigns. In: Agosti, M., Borbinha, J., Kapidakis, S., Papatheodorou, C., Tsakonas, G. (eds.) ECDL 2009. LNCS, vol. 5714, pp. 63–74. Springer, Heidelberg (2009)

17. Agosti, M., Ferro, N., Thanos, C.: DESIRE 2011: First international workshop on data infrastructures for supporting information retrieval evaluation. In: Proc. of the 20th ACM International Conference on Information and Knowledge Management, pp. 2631–2632. ACM, New York (2011)

18. Voorhees, E.M., Harman, D.K.: TREC: Experiment and Evaluation in Information Retrieval. The MIT Press, MA (2005)

19. Elmasri, R., Navathe, S.B.: Fundamentals of Database Systems, 4th edn. Addison Wesley, Reading (2003)

Penalty Functions for Evaluation Measures of Unsegmented Speech Retrieval

Petra Galuščáková, Pavel Pecina, and Jan Hajič

Institute of Formal and Applied Linguistics,
Faculty of Mathematics and Physics,
Charles University in Prague, Czech Republic
{galuscakova,pecina,hajic}@ufal.mff.cuni.cz

Abstract. This paper deals with evaluation of information retrieval from unsegmented speech. We focus on Mean Generalized Average Precision, the evaluation measure widely used for unsegmented speech retrieval. This measure is designed to allow certain tolerance in matching retrieval results (starting points of relevant segments) against a gold standard relevance assessment. It employs a Penalty Function which evaluates non-exact matches in the retrieval results based on their distance from the beginnings of their nearest true relevant segments. However, the choice of the Penalty Function is usually ad-hoc and does not necessary reflect users' perception of the speech retrieval quality. We perform a lab test to study satisfaction of users of a speech retrieval system to empirically estimate the optimal shape of the Penalty Function.

1 Introduction and Motivation

The quantity of speech data has been increasing rapidly in the last decades. Successful and efficient search in speech data requires the use of high-quality information retrieval (IR) systems which, in turn, are impossible to construct without reliable evaluation of the quality of these systems. IR from speech data (speech retrieval) differs substantially from IR from text documents (document retrieval) and thus special-purpose evaluation techniques are required.

Speech retrieval is defined as retrieving information from a collection of audio data (recordings) in response to a given query – modality of the query could be arbitrary, either text or speech. This task is usually being solved as text retrieval on transcriptions of the audio obtained by automatic speech recognition (ASR). IR systems reported being used for such speech retrieval are e.g. Lemur [11], SMART [10], Terrier [10] and InQuery [9].

Speech retrieval systems based on ASR must deal with a number of issues unknown to the traditional text retrieval: Automatic speech transcriptions are not 100% accurate and contain errors, i.e. misrecognized words. The vocabulary used in speech is usually different from the one used in written text (including colloquial and informal words [11], etc.). Speech contains additional elements such as word fragments, pause fillers, breath sounds, long pauses and it is usually not segmented into topically coherent passages, not even paragraphs or sentences.

T. Catarci et al. (Eds.): CLEF 2012, LNCS 7488, pp. 100–111, 2012.
© Springer-Verlag Berlin Heidelberg 2012

Evaluation of speech retrieval requires special measures designed specifically for this purpose. In this work, we focus on speech retrieval from recordings not segmented to passages which could serve as documents in the traditional IR. The main objective of this work is to verify whether the methods currently used for evaluation of speech retrieval in unsegmented recordings are appropriate and possibly modify these methods to better correspond to users' expectations. We focus on Mean Generalized Average Precision (mGAP) [7], which is de-facto standard measure for evaluation of unsegmented speech retrieval. mGAP has been used for several years but to our best knowledge such verification has not been reported yet. This work is the first attempt to do so.

First, we review evaluation of speech retrieval in general, then we describe a lab test carried out in order to measure satisfaction of the users with simulated results of a speech retrieval system. Based on an analysis of the survey results we propose a modification of the mGAP measure (or more precisely, its Penalty Function). Evaluation is performed on the results of the Cross-Language Speech-Retrieval track at CLEF 2007 [11], which includes a test collection, evaluation measure, and document rankings from the participating retrieval systems.

2 Evaluation of Speech Retrieval

The standard IR evaluation methods can be theoretically applied to speech retrieval but only if the speech collection is segmented to passages which can play the role of documents. If such a segmentation is not available, they cannot be used directly and need to be modified.

2.1 Segmented Speech Retrieval

In segmented speech retrieval, the collection consists of topically coherent passages which can be judged to be relevant or non-relevant to a particular query (or topic) as a whole. In that case, standard evaluation metrics, such as Mean Average Precision, can be used in the same way as for text document retrieval. This method was for example used in Unknown Story Boundaries Condition Track of TREC-8 [3], in which unknown boundaries of segments were converted to the known ones.

Precision (P) is defined as the ratio of the number of relevant retrieved documents to all retrieved documents and *Recall* (R) is the ratio of the number of relevant retrieved documents to all relevant documents. If an IR system also returns a relevance score for each retrieved document, these can be sorted in a descending order according to this score in a ranked list (for a given topic). For such a ranked list, one can compute the Average Precision (AP) as an arithmetic mean of the values of precision for the set of first m most relevant retrieved documents. This score is calculated for each new retrieved relevant document (d_m) [8]. Let S_k be the set of the first k retrieved documents for a given query and:

$$AP(d_m) = \frac{1}{m} \cdot \sum_{k=1}^{m} precision(S_k). \tag{1}$$

Mean Average Precision (MAP) is then calculated as an arithmetic mean of the AP values for the set of the queries Q on the set of documents D, formally:

$$MAP(Q) = \frac{1}{|Q|} \cdot \sum_{j=1}^{|Q|} AP_{Q_j}(D). \tag{2}$$

If no relevant document was retrieved, then the MAP value is equal to zero.

2.2   Unsegmented Speech Retrieval

If the collection consists of recordings with no topical segmentation, the system is expected to retrieve exact starting (and eventually ending) points of each passage relevant to a given query (or topic). The main issue with evaluation of such retrieval results is that failing to match a starting point exactly cannot be interpreted as a complete failure, which is the case in document retrieval.

Only a few measures targeting unsegmented speech retrieval have been proposed. Liu and Oard in [7] proposed the Mean Generalized Average Precision (mGAP) measure, a modification of MAP for unsegmented speech retrieval. This measure was used for example for the evaluation of Cross-Language Speech Retrieval Track of CLEF [10] and Rich Speech Retrieval Task of MediaEval Benchmark [6]. Eskevich et al. [2] introduced two measures for search in informally structured speech data: Mean Average Segment Precision (MASP) and Mean Average Segment Distance-Weighted Precision (MASDWP). MASP is a modification of MAP, inspired by MAiP [5] designed for evaluation of retrieval of relevant document parts. This measure evaluates retrieval systems with respect to segmentation quality and ranking of the results. MASDWP measure, similarly to mGAP, takes into account the distance between the start of a relevant segment and the retrieved segment [2], but employs segment precision too.

Mean Generalized Average Precision was designed to allow certain tolerance in matching search results (starting points of relevant segments) against a gold standard relevance assessment. This tolerance is determined by the Penalty Function, a function of the time difference between the starting point of the topic determined by the system and the true starting point of this topic obtained during relevance assessment. *Generalized Average Precision* is defined formally as:

$$GAP = \frac{\sum_{R_k \neq 0} p_k}{N}, \tag{3}$$

where N is the number of assessed starting points, R_k is a reward calculated according to the Penalty Function for the starting point retrieved on the position k and p_k is the value of Precision for the position k calculated as:

$$p_k = \frac{\sum_{i=1}^{k} R_i}{k}. \tag{4}$$

Each annotated point is used in the Penalty Function calculation only once.

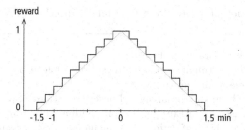

Fig. 1. mGAP Penalty Function used the CL-SR track at CLEF 2006 and 2007

mGAP is then defined analogically as in Equation (2) as an arithmetic mean of the values GAP for a set of queries Q and a set of documents D.

Values of Penalty Function are always non-negative and they decrease with increasing distance from the true starting points. For exact matches the Penalty Function returns 1 as a maximum reward. From a certain distance the function values are equal to zero. Apart from this, the actual shape of the function can be chosen arbitrarily. The Penalty Function used in the mGAP measure in the Cross-Language Speech Retrieval Track of CLEF 2006 [10] and 2007 [11] is shown in Figure 1. This function is not smooth, for each 9 seconds of time between the retrieved and true starting points the function decreases by 0.1. Thus, the interval for which the function gives non-zero scores is [-1.5,1.5] minutes.

The proposed mGAP measure has been widely used in recent evaluation campaigns [10,11] and research papers [4]. However, the measure (and the Penalty Function itself) have not been adequately studied as of yet. It is not clear to what extent mGAP scores correlate with human satisfaction of retrieval results.

For example, the Penalty Function is symmetrical and starting points retrieved by a system in the same distance before and after a true starting point are treated as equally good (or bad). We do not have enough empirical evidence whether this assumption is correct. Another point which needs to be verified is the "width" of the Penalty Function, i.e. the maximum distance for which the reward is non-zero, and the actual "shape" of the function itself.

The main purpose of the study is therefore to verify the appropriateness of the mGAP Penalty Function by examining the correlation of its scores and actual human behaviour and satisfaction in a simulated environment of a speech retrieval system.

3   Methodology

We have designed a lab test to study the behaviour of users when presented results of a speech retrieval system – i.e. a starting point of a segment which should be relevant to a particular topic. The users did not use a real speech retrieval system. Instead, they were presented a topic description and a starting point randomly generated in the vicinity of a starting point of a true relevant segment in an interface allowing basic playback functions. We measured a subjective satisfaction of the users with the retrieved starting point (whether it pointed to a

Table 1. Translation of a topic from the Malach speech-retrieval test collection

Id 1148	

Id 1148
Title Jewish resistance in Europe
Description Provide testimonies or describe actions of Jewish resistance in Europe before and during the war.
Narrative The relevant material should describe actions of only-or mostly Jewish resistance in Europe. Both individual and group-based actions are relevant. Type of actions may include survival (fleeing, hiding, saving children), testifying (alerting the outside world, writing, hiding testimonies), fighting (partisans, uprising, political security). Information about undifferentiated resistance groups is not relevant.

passage relevant to the given topic or not and/or how difficult it was to find one) and the time they spent doing this.

3.1 Test Collection

Data for the survey (including recordings, topic descriptions, and relevance assessments) was taken from the test collection [4] used for Cross-Language Speech-Retrieval track of the CLEF 2007 [11]. This collection was built from a part of oral history archive from the Malach Project[1]. This archive consists of 52,000 Holocaust survivors' testimonies in 32 languages. A subset of 357 testimonies recorded in Czech was manually processed by human assessors and passages relevant to 118 topics were identified for the purposes of the CLEF evaluation campaign. 32 topics were assessed by at least two assessors in parallel. The assessors identified 5 436 relevant segments with an average duration of 167 seconds. An example of a test topic is given in Table 1. The description consists of four parts – numerical ID, title, short description, and a more verbose narrative. All the topics are related Holocaust, Word War II, etc. An average length of a testimony in the test collection is approximately 95 min.

3.2 User Interface

For the purpose of our survey we have developed a custom user interface, implemented as an on-line application in the Flex programming language[2] to be easily used over the Internet (in a web browser). Participants of the survey did not have to download the application and data to their computers what reduced their effort. A screenshot of the interface is displayed in Figure 2.

The key component of the interface is an audio player which allows the survey participants to listen and navigate through the presented recordings. The interface also displays the topics. The player control buttons include the standard play and pause buttons, volume indicator, and a large slider for precise navigation in the recording, as well as buttons for fast forward and backward jump

---

[1] http://malach.umiacs.umd.edu
[2] http://www.adobe.com/products/flex.html

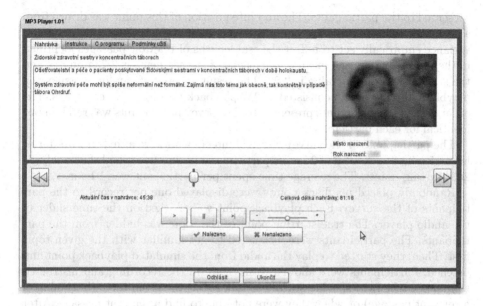

Fig. 2. A screenshot of the user interface used during the survey focused on behaviour of users analysing simulated results of a speech retrieval system

(by 30 seconds). The randomly generated starting points are indicated by a red icon on the slider (one at a time). When users identified a relevant passage they were instructed to press the "Found" ("Nalezeno") button below the control bar and indicate their level of satisfaction in a newly opened pop-up window. If the users were not satisfied with a presented starting point (and could not find a relevant passage nearby) they were allowed to proceed with the next starting point by pressing the "Not Found" ("Nenalezeno") button, but they could not return back. Some additional information was accessible through the interface: description of the topic being processed, details of the current speaker (picture and some basic information), survey instructions, etc. All actions of the participants, such as the movement of the slider, playing and stopping the record were recorded in order to study the behaviour of the participants. As all the data used in the survey were in Czech, the language of the interface was Czech too.

3.3   Survey

The survey was designed to simulate results of a retrieval system. The participants did not input any query; instead, they were presented the topics from the test collection and playback points randomly generated in a vicinity of a starting point of a relevant segment. The survey data was prepared as follows. First, we removed topics which were assessed by one assessor only and topics which had less than 5 assessed relevant segments. For each of the remaining topics, we randomly selected a set of seven relevant segments and their starting points. For each of the true starting points we randomly generated one simulated starting point which was

presented to the participants. The absolute position of this point was drawn from
a normal distribution with mean set to the position of the true starting point and
variance empirically set to reflect the real lengths of relevant passages identified
in the test collection: the mean of the length of the segments is 2.73 minutes and
the standard deviation value is 2.92. The resulting pool of randomly generated
playback starting points consisted of 257 playback times in 157 recordings. The
order of the playback points presented to the survey participants was random but
identical for each participant.

The participants of the survey were volunteers who were asked to work for at
least 15 minutes. A total of 24 users participated in the survey and they analysed
263 starting points. The average time spent per participant was 1 hour.

Randomly placed playback points were displayed one per record to the participants of the survey. Each playback point was marked on the time slider of
the audio player. The true starting point of the topic was hidden from the participants. The participants were instructed to get familiar with the given topic
first. Then, they started to play the audio from the simulated playback point and
listened. Participants were allowed to navigate in the recording and instructed
to indicate when the speaker started to talk about the given topic (beginning of
a relevant passage) or when they were not able to find a relevant passage. After
they found the relevant segment, the participants were asked to indicate their
satisfaction with the playback point (how easy it was to find a beginning of a
relevant passage) on a four-point scale: *very good*, *good*, *bad*, and *very bad.*

4   Results

As we have mentioned earlier, we consider two factors as indicators of the quality
of the (simulated) retrieval results: a) the time needed to find the starting point
of a passage relevant to the given topic and b) the overall satisfaction with the
retrieval result (i.e. the location of the playback point). This allows us to analyse
correlation of these two factors with the relative position of the starting point
of the true relevant passages.

4.1   Time Analysis

Time needed for finding the relevant information is an important measure of
quality of an IR system [1]. In our user study, we measure the elapsed time between the beginning of playback and the moment when the participant presses
the button indicating that the relevant passage was found. Figure 3 visualizes
these values on the vertical axis with respect to the difference between the simulated playback points and true starting points on the horizontal axis.

The key observation is that the respondents generally need less time to complete the task when the playback point is located *before* the true starting point.
For the playback points generated 3 minutes before the true starting point the

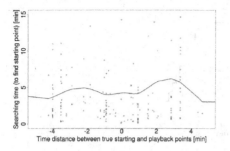

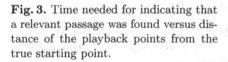

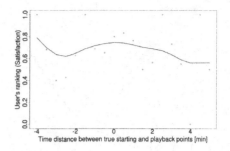

Fig. 3. Time needed for indicating that a relevant passage was found versus distance of the playback points from the true starting point.

Fig. 4. Average retrieval satisfaction of respondents versus distance of the playback starting points from the true starting points.

average time needed to find the relevant segment is 1.7 minutes. For the playback points generated 3 minutes after the true starting point the average time needed to find the relevant segment is 2.1 minutes. With increasing distance from the true starting points the situation changes. The average time needed to find a relevant segment is 3 minutes when the playback point lies 5 minutes before the true starting point and 2.6 minutes when the playback point lies 5 minutes after starting point. However, this is very biased by a number of cases when the respondents gave up searching the relevant passages at all. There were 68 such cases (26%) and most of them happened when the generated playback points appeared 5 to 3 minutes before the true starting point.

When a playback point is placed closer than one minute to the true starting point, the time needed to mark the starting point is almost the same as if the playback reference and true starting points were coincident. When the time between true starting and reference points is more than four minutes, the values are distorted due to the smaller number of observations.

4.2   Users' Satisfaction

The second aspect is the overall (subjective) satisfaction with the playback points in terms of retrieval quality. During the survey, participants were requested to indicate to what extent they were happy with the location of the playback points in the scale of: *very good, good, bad* or *very bad*. This scale was then transformed into real number values: the responses *very good* and *good* were assigned 1, and *bad* and *very bad* were assigned 0. The cases in which no starting point was found were treated as *very bad* and assigned 0. Then the arithmetic mean of these values from all respondents was calculated for each generated playback point. Visualization of the results is shown in Figure 4.

The trend of the spline function generated from the satisfaction values is not clear. The respondents seem to be most satisfied when the playback reference point lies shortly before the true starting point (negative values). On the other

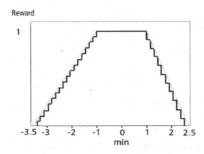

Fig. 5. The proposed modification of Penalty Function

hand, the function value decreases more slowly for positive time when the playback point lies after the true starting point. This means that if a starting point is retrieved, for example, two minutes after the true starting point it is likely that the speaker is still talking about the topic, the participant could guess where the topic starts and he/she judges the retrieval result to be better. This stands against the results of the time needed to mark the starting point, though.

5 Proposed mGAP Modifications

If we want to propose a modification of the mGAP Penalty Function which would better reflect user perception of speech retrieval quality, the following findings of the user study should be taken into account:

1. Users prefer playback points appearing before the beginning of a true relevant passages to those appearing after, i.e. more reward should be given to playback points appearing before the true starting point of a relevant segment (negative time distance).
2. Users are tolerant to playback points appearing within a 1-minute distance from the true starting points. i.e. equal (maximum) reward should be given to all playback points which are closer than one minute to the true starting point.
3. Users are still satisfied when playback points appear in two- or three- minute distance from the true starting point. i.e. function should be "wider".

Our proposal of the modified mGAP Penalty Function based on these findings is shown in Figure 5. The "width" of this new function for positive time values is 2.5 minutes. This time corresponds to the average length of a speaker's talk on one topic in Malach data collection[3]. The average length of the topic may differ for various collections. Therefore, the possibility of arranging this time according to the recordings collection specification should be further studied. Because of the better results of the points in negative time we enlarged the width of this function in the negative time region to 3.5 minutes. We decided not to take into

---

[3] This information comes from the data used in the CLEF evaluation campaign.

Table 2. mGAP scores of the retrieval systems participating in the CLEF 2007 CL-SR track calculated with original and modified Penalty Functions.

Submission	Team	Orig. PF	Modif. PF	Difference
UWB_2-1_tdn_l	University of West Bohemia	0.0274	0.0490	0.0216
UWB_3-1_tdn_l	University of West Bohemia	0.0241	0.0517	0.0276
UWB_2-1_td_s	University of West Bohemia	0.0229	0.0383	0.0154
UCcsaTD2	University of Chicago	0.0213	0.0387	0.0174
UCcslTD1	University of Chicago	0.0196	0.0359	0.0163
prague04	Charles University in Prague	0.0195	0.0373	0.0178
prague01	Charles University in Prague	0.0192	0.0370	0.0178
prague02	Charles University in Prague	0.0183	0.0347	0.0164
UWB_3-1_td_l	University of West Bohemia	0.0134	0.0256	0.0122
UWB_2-1_td_w	University of West Bohemia	0.0132	0.0255	0.0123
UCunstTD3	University of Chicago	0.0126	0.0270	0.0144
brown.s.f	Brown University	0.0113	0.0258	0.0145
brown.sA.f	Brown University	0.0106	0.0242	0.0136
prague03	Charles University in Prague	0.0098	0.0208	0.011
brown.f	Brown University	0.0049	0.0131	0.0082

account the fact that users prefer playback points lying before starting points of true relevant segments in a greater distance. Starting point retrieved closer than one minute to the true starting point is considered to be equally good as exact match. This reflects the tolerance of smaller nuances in retrieval which are difficult to recognize even by a human.

The reward assigned by the modified Penalty Function will always be higher than the one from the original Penalty Function. Consequently, the mGAP score calculated using the proposed function will be higher too.

5.1   Comparison with the Original Measure

We evaluate the impact of the proposed modification of the Penalty Function in the setting of the CLEF 2007 Cross-Language Speech Retrieval Track [11]. We have rescored all 15 retrieval systems which participated in the task using mGAP with the modified Penalty Function and we have compared the results with the original scores, see Table 2. Visual comparison is then shown in Figure 6.

The original and new scores are quite correlated, the final rankings of the retrieval systems differ only in a few cases and the absolute changes are relatively small and not significant. The high correlation is mainly caused by the large amount of cases in which is the Penalty Function equal to 0: Almost 98% of all Penalty Function values are equal to 0. Figure 7 illustrates in how many cases the scoring (reward) of individual retrieved points actually changed when the modified Penalty Function was applied. This nicely corresponds with the modified shape of the Penalty Function.

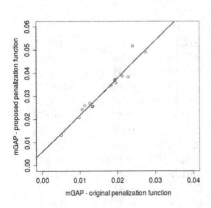

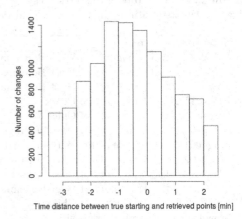

Fig. 6. Comparison of the scores calculated by mGAP with original and modified Penalty Function.

Fig. 7. Distribution of reward changes using the original and modified penalty function on the CL-SR CLEF 2007 results.

6   Conclusion

We have examined metrics used for evaluation of information retrieval from speech recordings. Our main focus was on the mGAP measure, which is currently often used for retrieval of unsegmented recordings. Several drawbacks of this measure were described and an experiment to help to improve this measure was proposed. At the core of the experiment was a human-based lab test in which participants were asked to search for the starting point of a particular topic. A total of 24 respondents participated in this test. A modified Penalty Function to be used in the mGAP measure was proposed based on our test results. The three most significant modifications to the original Penalty Function are that the new Penalty function is "wider" than the original one, the new Penalty Function prefers IR systems which retrieve a topic starting point before the true annotated starting point and if the IR system retrieves a starting point closer than one minute from the annotated point, there is no penalty. Finally, a comparison of the original and modified Penalty Functions was performed using real data from retrieval systems used in CLEF 2007 track and a high correlation between the outputs of the mGAP measure with the two Penalty Functions has been found. As a result, the original ranking of retrieval system from CL-SR CLEF 2007 changed only insignificantly.

Acknowledgements. This research was supported by the project AMALACH (grant no. DF12P01OVV022 of the program NAKI of the Ministry of Culture of the Czech Republic), the Czech Science Foundation (grant n. P103/12/G084) and SVV project number 265 314.

References

1. Cleverdon, C.W., Mills, J., Keen, M.: Factors determining the performance of indexing systems. Test results, vol. 2. Aslib Cranfield Research Project, Cranfield, England (1966)
2. Eskevich, M., Magdy, W., Jones, G.J.F.: New Metrics for Meaningful Evaluation of Informally Structured Speech Retrieval. In: Baeza-Yates, R., de Vries, A.P., Zaragoza, H., Cambazoglu, B.B., Murdock, V., Lempel, R., Silvestri, F. (eds.) ECIR 2012. LNCS, vol. 7224, pp. 170–181. Springer, Heidelberg (2012)
3. Garofolo, J., Auzanne, C., Ellen, V., Sparck, J.K.: 1999 TREC-8 Spoken Document Retrieval (SDR) Track Evaluation Specification (1999), http://www.itl.nist.gov/iad/mig/tests/sdr/1999/spec.html
4. Ircing, P., Pecina, P., Oard, D.W., Wang, J., White, R.W., Hoidekr, J.: Information Retrieval Test Collection for Searching Spontaneous Czech Speech. In: Matoušek, V., Mautner, P. (eds.) TSD 2007. LNCS (LNAI), vol. 4629, pp. 439–446. Springer, Heidelberg (2007)
5. Kamps, J., Pehcevski, J., Kazai, G., Lalmas, M., Robertson, S.: INEX 2007 Evaluation Measures. In: Fuhr, N., Kamps, J., Lalmas, M., Trotman, A. (eds.) INEX 2007. LNCS, vol. 4862, pp. 24–33. Springer, Heidelberg (2008)
6. Larson, M., Eskevich, M., Ordelman, R., Kofler, C., Schmiedeke, S., Jones, G.J.F.: Overview of MediaEval 2011 rich speech retrieval task and genre tagging task. In: Larson, M., Rae, A., Demarty, C.H., Kofler, C., Metze, F., Troncy, R., Mezaris, V., Jones, G.J.F. (eds.) Working Notes Proceedings of the MediaEval 2011 Workshop. CEUR Workshop Proceedings, vol. 807, pp. 1–2. CEUR-WS.org (2011)
7. Liu, B., Oard, D.W.: One-sided measures for evaluating ranked retrieval effectiveness with spontaneous conversational speech. In: Proceedings of the 29th Annual International ACM SIGIR Conference on Research and Development in Information Retrieval, SIGIR 2006, pp. 673–674. ACM, New York (2006)
8. Manning, C.D., Raghavan, P., Schütze, H.: Introduction to Information Retrieval. Cambridge University Press, New York (2008)
9. Oard, D.W., Hackett, P.G.: Document Translation for Cross-Language Text Retrieval at the University of Maryland. In: Voorhees, E.M., Harman, D.K. (eds.) The Sixth Text REtrieval Conference (TREC-6), pp. 687–696. U.S. Dept. of Commerce, Technology Administration, National Institute of Standards and Technology (1997)
10. Oard, D.W., Wang, J., Jones, G.J.F., White, R.W., Pecina, P., Soergel, D., Huang, X., Shafran, I.: Overview of the CLEF-2006 Cross-Language Speech Retrieval Track. In: Peters, C., Clough, P., Gey, F.C., Karlgren, J., Magnini, B., Oard, D.W., de Rijke, M., Stempfhuber, M. (eds.) CLEF 2006. LNCS, vol. 4730, pp. 744–758. Springer, Heidelberg (2007)
11. Pecina, P., Hoffmannová, P., Jones, G.J.F., Zhang, Y., Oard, D.W.: Overview of the CLEF-2007 Cross-Language Speech Retrieval Track. In: Peters, C., Jijkoun, V., Mandl, T., Müller, H., Oard, D.W., Peñas, A., Petras, V., Santos, D. (eds.) CLEF 2007. LNCS, vol. 5152, pp. 674–686. Springer, Heidelberg (2008)

Cumulated Relative Position:
A Metric for Ranking Evaluation

Marco Angelini[3], Nicola Ferro[1], Kalervo Järvelin[2], Heikki Keskustalo[2],
Ari Pirkola[2], Giuseppe Santucci[3], and Gianmaria Silvello[1]

[1] University of Padua, Italy
{ferro,silvello}@dei.unipd.it
[2] University of Tampere, Finland
{kalervo.jarvelin,heikki.keskustalo,ari.pirkola}@uta.fi
[3] "La Sapienza" University of Rome, Italy
{angelini,santucci}@dis.uniroma1.it

Abstract. The development of multilingual and multimedia information access systems calls for proper evaluation methodologies to ensure
that they meet the expected user requirements and provide the desired
effectiveness. IR research offers a strong evaluation methodology and a
range of evaluation metrics, such as MAP and (n)DCG. In this paper, we
propose a new metric for ranking evaluation, the CRP. We start with the
observation that a document of a given degree of relevance may be ranked
too early or too late regarding the ideal ranking of documents for a query.
Its relative position may be negative, indicating too early ranking, zero
indicating correct ranking, or positive, indicating too late ranking. By
cumulating these relative rankings we indicate, at each ranked position,
the net effect of document displacements, the CRP. We first define the
metric formally and then discuss its properties, its relationship to prior
metrics, and its visualization. Finally we propose different visualizations
of CRP by exploiting a test collection to demonstrate its behavior.

1 Introduction

Designing, developing, and evaluating an *Information Retrieval (IR)* system is a
challenging task, especially when it comes to understanding and analyzing the
behavior of the system under different conditions in order to tune or to improve
it as to achieve the level of effectiveness needed to meet the user expectations.

The development of information access systems calls for proper evaluation
methodologies to ensure that they meet the expected user requirements and provide the desired effectiveness. IR research offers a strong evaluation methodology based on test collections [1]. A range of evaluation metrics, such as MAP and
nDCG, are widely used within this methodology [2]. These metrics are particularly
suitable to the evaluation of IR techniques in terms of the quality of the output
ranked lists, and often to some degree suitable to the evaluation of user experience
regarding retrieval. Unfortunately, the traditional metrics do not take deviations

T. Catarci et al. (Eds.): CLEF 2012, LNCS 7488, pp. 112–123, 2012.

from optimal document ranking sufficiently into account. For example, the *Mean Average Precision (MAP)* only considers precision at relevant document ranks and employs binary relevance. MAP nor its extensions to graded relevance [3,4] offer no explicit method for penalizing for suboptimal documents ranked early. Further, the original *Normalized Discounted Cumulated Gain ((n)DCG)* [5] only discounts the relevance gain of late-arriving relevant documents without penalizing for suboptimal documents ranked early. While the extension of (n)DCG [6] penalizes for retrieving non-relevant documents, it does not generally handle ranking suboptimal documents early and does not explicitly take into account the severity of document mis-ranking. We think that a proper evaluation metric for ranked result lists in IR should: (a) explicitly handle graded relevance including negative gains for unhelpful documents, and (b) explicitly take into account document mis-placements in ranking either too early or too late given their degree of relevance and the optimal ranking. In the present paper, we propose such a new evaluation metric, the *Cumulated Relative Position (CRP)*.

We start with the observation that a document of a given degree of relevance may be ranked too early or too late regarding the ideal ranking of documents for a query. Its relative position may be negative, indicating too early ranking, zero indicating correct ranking, or positive, indicating too late ranking. By cumulating these relative rankings we indicate, at each ranked position, the net effect of document displacements, the CRP.

The novel CRP metric is related to prior metrics, such as sliding ratio [7], normalized recall [7,8], the satisfaction frustration total measure [7], and (n)DCG. However, CRP differs from these in explicitly handling: (a) graded relevance, and (b) document misplacements either too early or too late given their degree of relevance and the ideal ranking. Thereby, CRP offers several advantages in IR evaluation:

- at any number of retrieved documents examined (rank) for a given query, it is obvious to interpret and it gives an estimate of ranking performance as a single measure relative to the ideal ranking for the topic;
- it is not dependent on outliers since it focuses on the ranking of the result list;
- it is directly user-oriented in reporting the deviation from ideal ranking when examining a given number of documents; the effort wasted in examining a suboptimal ranking is made explicit;
- it allows conflation of relevance grades of documents and therefore more or less fine-grained analyses of the ranking performance of an IR technique may be produced;
- it can be summarized by four synthesis indicators describing the ranking quality of the IR system under investigation;
- it is possible to point out several graphical representations by stressing one of the different aspects of measurement allowed by CRP.

The rest of the paper is organized as follows: Section 2 presents the CRP and its properties. Section 3 presents a comparison between CRP and previous metrics and considerations about their ability of addressing the bi-directional nature of search results. Section 4 presents a visualization of the CRP by comparing it with the DCG and a visualization of the CRP synthesis indicators based on parallel coordinates. Lastly, Section 5 draws some final remarks and points-out future developments of CRP.

2   Cumulated Relative Position

2.1   Definition of the Metric

We define the set of *relevance degrees* as $(REL, \leq)$ such that there is an order between the elements of REL. For example, for the set $REL = \{\mathtt{nr}, \mathtt{pr}, \mathtt{fr}, \mathtt{hr}\}$, $\mathtt{nr}$ stands for "non relevant", $\mathtt{pr}$ for "partially relevant", $\mathtt{fr}$ for "fairly relevant", $\mathtt{hr}$ stands for "highly relevant", and it holds $\mathtt{nr} \leq \mathtt{pr} \leq \mathtt{fr} \leq \mathtt{hr}$.

We define a function RW : $REL \to \mathbb{Z}$ as a monotonic function[1] which maps each relevance degree $(rel \in REL)$ into an *relevance weight* $(w_{rel} \in \mathbb{Z})$, e.g. $\mathrm{RW}(\mathtt{hr}) = 3$. This function allows us to associate an integer number to a relevance degree; much of the previous work studied the impact of varying these weights on *Cumulated Gain (CG)*, *Discounted Cumulated Gain (DCG)*, and (n)DCG measures [5,6].

We define with D the set of documents we take into account, with $N \in \mathbb{N}$ a natural number, and with D^N the set of all possible vectors of length N containing different orderings of the documents in D. We can also say that a vector in D^N represents a ranking list of length N of the documents D retrieved by an IR system. Let us consider a vector $\mathbf{v} \in D^N$, a natural number $j \in [1, N]$, and a relevance degree $rel \in REL$, then the *ground truth* function is defined as:

$$\begin{aligned} \mathrm{GT} : D^N \times \mathbb{N} \to REL \\ \mathbf{v}[j] \mapsto rel \end{aligned} \tag{1}$$

Equation 1 allows us to associate a relevance degree to the document $d \in D$ retrieved at position j of the vector $\mathbf{v}$, i.e. it associates a relevance judgment to each retrieved document in a ranked list.

In the following, we define with $\mathbf{r} \in D^N$ the vector of documents retrieved and ranked by a run r, with $\mathbf{i} \in D^N$ the ideal vector containing the best ranking of the documents in the pool (e.g. all highly relevant documents are grouped together in the beginning of the vector followed by fairly relevant ones and so on and so forth), and with $\mathbf{w} \in D^N$ the worst-case vector containing the worst rank of the documents retrieved by the pool (e.g. all the relevant documents are put in the end of the vector in the inverse relevance order).

In the following we use an example to explain the equations we introduce. Let us consider an ideal vector $\mathbf{i}$ composed of k intervals of documents sharing the same rel. We assume to have a pool composed by 20 elements where $k = 4$ and the recall base is $R = 10$. Let $\mathbf{i}$ be $[\mathtt{hr}, \mathtt{hr}, \mathtt{hr}, \mathtt{fr}, \mathtt{fr}, \mathtt{fr}, \mathtt{pr}, \mathtt{pr}, \mathtt{pr}, \mathtt{pr}, \mathtt{nr}, \dots, \mathtt{nr}]$. The worst-case vector $\mathbf{w}$ is $[\mathtt{nr}, \dots, \mathtt{nr}, \mathtt{pr}, \mathtt{pr}, \mathtt{pr}, \mathtt{pr}, \mathtt{fr}, \mathtt{fr}, \mathtt{fr}, \mathtt{hr}, \mathtt{hr}, \mathtt{hr}]$. Then, let us consider two systems A and B such that:

---

[1] This means that $\forall \{rel_1, rel_2\} \in REL \mid rel_1 \leq rel_2 \Rightarrow \mathrm{RW}(rel_1) \leq \mathrm{RW}(rel_2)$.

$$r_A = [hr, hr, fr, nr, pr, fr, nr, nr, nr, pr, hr, nr, \ldots, nr]$$
$$r_B = [hr, hr, pr, nr, fr, pr, nr, nr, fr, pr, fr, nr, hr, pr, nr, \ldots, nr]$$

The recall of system A is $\frac{7}{10}$, whereas the recall of system B is 1.

From function GT we can point out a set called *relevance support* defined as:

$$RS(\mathbf{v}, rel) = \{j \in [1, N] \mid GT(\mathbf{v}, j) = rel\} \tag{2}$$

which, given a vector $\mathbf{v} \in D^N$ – it can be a run vector $\mathbf{r}$, the ideal vector $\mathbf{i}$, or the worst-case vector $\mathbf{w}$ – and a relevance degree rel, contains the indexes j of the documents of $\mathbf{v}$ with which the given relevance degree (rel) relevance is associated. For instance, in the presented example we have $RS(r_A, hr) = \{1, 2, 11\}$ and $RS(r_B, hr) = \{1, 2, 3\}$.

Given the ideal vector $\mathbf{i}$ and a relevance degree rel, we can define the *minimum rank* in $\mathbf{i}$ as the first position in which we find a document with relevance degree equal to rel. In the same way, we can define the *maximum rank* in $\mathbf{i}$ as the last position in which we find a document with relevance degree equal to rel. In formulas, they become:

$$\min_i(rel) = \min\left(RS(\mathbf{i}, rel)\right)$$
$$\max_i(rel) = \max\left(RS(\mathbf{i}, rel)\right) \tag{3}$$

In the context of our example, we can say that : $\min_i(hr) = 1$, $\max_i(hr) = 3$, $\min_i(fr) = 4$, $\max_i(fr) = 6$, $\min_i(pr) = 7$, $\max_i(pr) = 10$, $\min_i(nr) = 11$, and $\max_i(nr) = 20$.

Given a vector $\mathbf{v}$ and a document at position $j \in [1, N]$, we can define the *Relative Position (RP)* as:

$$RP(\mathbf{v}, j) = \begin{cases} 0 & \text{if } \min_i\left(GT(\mathbf{v}, j)\right) \leq j \leq \max_i\left(GT(\mathbf{v}, j)\right) \\ j - \min_i(GT(\mathbf{v}, j)) & \text{if } j < \min_i\left(GT(\mathbf{v}, j)\right) \\ j - \max_i(GT(\mathbf{v}, j)) & \text{if } j > \max_i\left(GT(\mathbf{v}, j)\right) \end{cases} \tag{4}$$

RP allows for pointing out misplaced documents and understanding how much they are misplaced with respect to the ideal case $\mathbf{i}$. Zero values denote documents which are within the ideal interval, positive values denote documents which are ranked below their ideal interval, and negative values denote documents which are above their ideal interval. Note that the greater the absolute value of $RP(\mathbf{v}, j)$ is, the bigger is the distance of the document at position j from its ideal interval. From equation 4, it follows that $RP(\mathbf{i}, j) = 0, \forall j \in [1, N]$.

In our example we can determine the following RP vectors:

$$RP(r_A) = [0, 0, -1, -7, -2, 0, -4, -3, -2, 0, +8, 0, \ldots, 0]$$

$$RP(r_B) = [0, 0, -4, -7, 0, -1, -4, -3, +3, 0, +5, 0, +10, +4, 0, \ldots, 0]$$

Given a vector $\mathbf{v}$ and a document at position $j \in [1, N]$, we can define the *Cumulated Relative Position (CRP)* as:

$$\mathrm{CRP}(\mathbf{v}, j) = \sum_{k=1}^{j} \mathrm{RP}(\mathbf{v}, k) \tag{5}$$

For each position j, CRP sums the values of RP up to position j included. From equation 5, it follows that $\mathrm{CRP}(\mathbf{i}, j) = 0, \forall j \in [1, N]$. In our example, $\mathrm{CRP}(\mathbf{r_A}, 20) = -11$ and $\mathrm{CRP}(\mathbf{r_B}, 20) = +3$.

2.2 Properties of the Metric

We can point out the following properties for CRP:

- CRP can only be zero or negative before reaching the rank of the recall base (R);
- the faster the CRP curve goes down before R, the worse the run is;
- after R the CRP curve is non-decreasing;
- after that the last relevant document has been encountered, CRP remains constant;
- the sooner we reach the x-axis (balance point: $b_{\mathbf{r}}$), the better the run is.

In Figure 1 we can see a sketch of the CRP for a topic of a run. For a given topic there are two fixed values which are the rank of recall base (R) and the number of retrieved documents (N); this allows us to compare systems on the R basis.

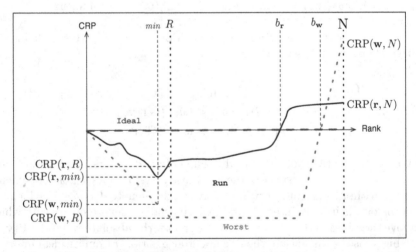

Fig. 1. Cumulative Relative Position sketch for a topic of a given run: min is the rank of the turn-around point of the run, R is the rank of the recall base, b_r is the rank of the balance point of the run, b_w is the rank of the balance point of the worst-case, N indicates the number of retrieved documents, $\mathrm{CRP}(\mathbf{r}, R)$ is the loss value of the run at R, $\mathrm{CRP}(\mathbf{r}, min)$ is the minimum CRP value of the run, $CRP(\mathbf{w}, min)$ is the CRP value of the worst-case at the minimum CRP of the run, $CRP(\mathbf{w}, R)$ is the loss value of the worst-case at R, $\mathrm{CRP}(\mathbf{w}, N)$ is the maximum CRP value of the worst-case, and $\mathrm{CRP}(\mathbf{r}, N)$ is the maximum CRP value of the run.

There are significant points both on the y-axis and in the x-axes. Given the run r, in the y-axes we point out three values:

1. $CRP(r, R)$: the **loss value** of the run measured at R;
2. $CRP(r, min)$: the minimum CRP of the run;
3. $CRP(r, N)$: the CRP value at N, it is the maximum value of CRP for the run.

In the x-axes we point out two points:

1. min: the **turn-around** point of the CRP curve, which is the most relevant point of inflection of the curve[2];
2. b_r: the **balance point** of the curve. It indicates the point where CRP has re-gained the value lost from 1 to min.

We can define four synthesis indicators describing the CRP curve of a topic for a given run. These indicators characterize the CRP curve and allow us to understand the behaviour of the system under examination for a given topic. Furthermore, these indicators are exploited to produce alternative visualizations of CRP; we can exploit them to read the CRP along different dimensions, each one representing a different aspect of the measurement.

The first indicator is the *recovery value* (ρ) defined as the ratio between R and b_r:

$$\rho = \frac{R}{b_r} \tag{6}$$

The recovery-value is always between 0 and 1 ($0 < \rho \leq 1$) where $\rho = 1$ indicates a perfect ranking and $\rho \to 0$ a progressively worse ranking. Please note that $\rho \to 0$ when $b_r \to \infty$.

The second indicator is the *balance ratio* (b_{ratio}) defined as *one* minus the ratio between b_r (i.e. balance point of the run) and b_w (i.e. balance point of the worst-case):

$$b_{ratio} = 1 - \frac{b_r}{b_w} \tag{7}$$

The balance ratio is always between 0 and 1 ($0 \leq b_{ratio} < 1$) where $b_{ratio} = 0$ indicates the worst possible ranking because $b_r = b_w$ and $b_{ratio} \to 1$ a progressively better ranking. Basically, the b_{ratio} points out the correlation between the ranking of the run and the worst-case ranking.

The third indicator is the minimum CRP value ratio (CRP_{min}) defined as *one* minus the ratio between the minimum CRP value of the run and the CRP value of the worst-case calculated in correspondence with the minimum CRP value of the run (please see Figure 1).

$$CRP_{min} = 1 - \frac{CRP(r, min)}{CRP(w, min)} \tag{8}$$

---

[2] An inflection point is a point on a curve at which the sign of the curvature (i.e., the concavity) changes.

The minimum CRP value ratio is always between 0 and 1 ($0 \leq \text{CRP}_{min} \leq 1$) where $\text{CRP}_{min} = 1$ indicates a perfect ranking because it means that $R = min$ and that $\text{CRP}(\mathbf{r}, min) = 0 = \text{CRP}(\mathbf{i}, min)$; on the other hand, $\text{CRP}_{min} = 0$ indicates the worst possible ranking because it means that $\text{CRP}(\mathbf{r}, min) = \text{CRP}(\mathbf{w}, min)$.

The fourth indicator is the CRP value ratio at N (CRP_N) defined as *one* minus the ratio between the CRP value at N of the run and the CRP value of the worst-case at N (please see Figure 1).

$$\text{CRP}_N = 1 - \frac{\text{CRP}(\mathbf{r}, N)}{\text{CRP}(\mathbf{w}, N)} \tag{9}$$

The CRP value ratio at N is always between 0 and 1 ($0 \leq \text{CRP}_N \leq 1$) where $\text{CRP}_N = 1$ indicates a good ranking because it means that $\text{CRP}(\mathbf{r}, N) = 0$, and $\text{CRP}_N = 0$ indicates the worst possible ranking because it means that $\text{CRP}(\mathbf{r}, N) = \text{CRP}(\mathbf{w}, N)$.

We consider an IR system which produces a set of runs defined as $RUN = \{\mathbf{r_1}, \mathbf{r_2}, \ldots, \mathbf{r_T}\}$ where $T \in \mathbb{N}$ is the number of considered topics; every topic has its own recall base R, so for topic t_1 there is a recall base R_1, for topic t_2 there is a recall base R_2 and so on and so forth until topic t_T with recall base R_T. Now, we can define the average recovery-value (ρ_{avg}) as:

$$\rho_{avg} = \frac{1}{T} \sum_{t=1}^{T} \frac{R_t}{b_{\mathbf{r_t}}} \tag{10}$$

The closer ρ_{avg} is to one, the better the system under examination behaves.

3   Comparison with Previous Metrics

The novel CRP metric has several advantages when compared with several previous and related measures. The *Normalized Recall (NR)* metric [8], the *Sliding Ratio (SR)* metric [7], and the *Satisfaction–Frustration–Total (SFT)* metric [7] all seek to take into account the order in which documents are presented to the user. The NR metric compares the actual performance of an IR technique to the ideal one (when all relevant documents are retrieved first). Basically, it measures the area between the ideal and the actual curves. NR does not take the degree of document relevance into account and is highly sensitive to the last relevant document found late in the ranked order.

The SR metric takes the degree of document relevance into account and actually computes the cumulated gain and normalizes this by the ideal cumulated gain for the same retrieval result. The result thus is quite similar to the *Normalized Cumulated Gain ((n)CG)* metric (see below). SR is dependent on the retrieved list size: with a longer list the ideal ranking may change essentially and this affects all values of the metric from rank one onwards. Improving on normalized recall, SR is not dependent on outliers, but it is sensitive to the actual retrieved set size.

The SFT metric consists of three components similar to the SR measure. The satisfaction metric only considers the retrieved relevant documents, the frustration metric only the irrelevant documents, and the total metric is a weighted combination of the two. Like SR, also SFT assumes equally long lists of retrieved documents, which are obtained in different orders by the IR techniques to be compared. This is a critical assumption for comparison since for any retrieved list size n, when $n << N$ (the database size), different IR techniques may retrieve quite different documents. A strong feature of SFT comes from its capability of penalizing an IR technique for retrieving irrelevant documents while rewarding for the relevant ones. CRP allows for comparison of equally long list of retrieved documents (e.g. n) by exploiting the $CRP(\mathbf{v}, n)$ value; but, at the same time it allows for comparisons based on the recall base (i.e. the recovery value) which are – to a reasonable degree – independent by the retrieved list size.

The cumulated gain–based metrics, the CG, DCG, (n)CG and (n)DCG [5], give at any rank examined, an estimate of the (normalized, discounted) cumulated gain as a single figure no matter what the recall base size is. They are not heavily dependent on relevant documents found late in the ranked order since they focus on the gain cumulated from the beginning of the result up to any point of interest. The discounted versions realistically weight down the gain received through documents found later in the ranked results. However, the gain values grow monotonically unless negative gain values [6] are used. The metrics do not explicitly handle ranking suboptimal documents early – this only shows lower gain values. Like the CRP, the normalized versions compare the ranking quality to each topics entire recall base (qrel) allowing statistical comparability.

Both the CRP and the CG-based metrics with negative weights address the issue of suboptimal ranking of search results but in different ways. The CRP indicates suboptimal ranking directly through the CRP curve; when this curve deviates from the X-axis (representing ideal ranking), ranking is suboptimal and less relevant documents are retrieved earlier than they should. The CG-based metrics do not directly address ranking optimality but cumulate gain and loss (or negative gain). Both metrics address the bi-directional nature of searching which may be seen as a process alternating between success and failure.

In traditional test collection-based evaluation, the evaluation task is simplified by abstracting away users, their situations and tasks [9], and relevance is assumed as topical, stable and binary. This neglects user experiences in real life with dynamic, multiple-dimension and multi-graded relevance [10,11] and user experiences caused by browsing sequences of non-relevant or suboptimal documents. Keskustalo and colleagues [6] analyze negative aspects in higher-order (above topical) relevance e.g. due to suboptimal ranking:

- Cognitive relevance: Not receiving pertinent information;
- situational relevance: Time pressure, effort;
- motivational/Affective relevance: Frustration, lack of accomplishment.

Both the CRP and the CG-based metrics, in particular their visualizations, facilitate the identification and analysis of these higher-order aspects of relevance. The dips in both kinds of graphs make this explicit in retrieval context (see Figure 2).

4   Experiments and Visualization

For the experimental analysis we adopted a test collection based on data from the TREC7 Ad-hoc test collection. A subset of all the *topics* 351-400 is considered, specifically those re-assessed in [5]. Indeed, the *relevance judgments* adopted are those obtained by the evaluation activity carried out in that paper. All the relevant documents of 20 TREC7 topics and 18 TREC8 topics were re-assessed together with 5% of documents judged as not relevant, where assessment was performed using a four graded relevance scale; details on the re-assessment procedure can be found in [12]. We developed a visual analytics prototype to visualize and interact with the various metrics adopted. In particular, we build on a first version of this prototype described in [13] to add the CRP visualizations. Figure 2 shows a screen shot of the running prototype comparing the CRP curve with the DCG curve (with negative weights).

For what it is concerned with CRP, the visualization prototype focuses on three types of visualization: (1) the "CRP Graph" which shows the trend of the CRP curve calculated on a specific topic for a given run (Figure 2a); (2) the "CRP Aggregate Graph" which shows, in a Parallel Coordinates fashion (a visualization technique well-suited to give an insight on the correlation of various measures on a big collection of data), an aggregate view of all the topics for the given run, ordered by their recall base rank (R) (Figure 3); and (3) the "CRP vs DCG Graph" which eases the comparison of the CRP curve and the DCG curve (Figure 2).

For this analysis we consider the run named "bbn1" submitted to the TREC7 Ad-Hoc Track [14]. Figure 2a shows the CRP curve for topic 351 of "bb1". Both the ideal and run curve are reported; please note that the ideal curve coincides with the x-axis. In the bottom part of the graph an horizontal bar shows the RP values; this bar helps the analyst to understand the single contribution of each document

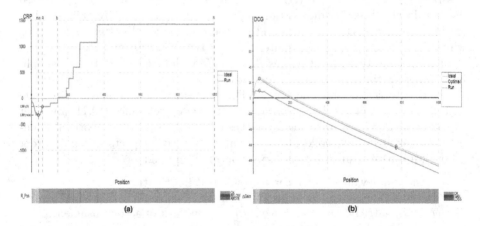

Fig. 2. Comparison between (a) CRP and (b) DCG with negative weights (i.e. $-1, 1, 2, 3$), on topic 351 of the "bb1" run.

to the CRP. The points corresponding to the synthesis indicators are reported to highlight the trend of the run and to pinpoint the areas in which the trend changes.

The visualization reported in Figure 2 allows the comparison, for the same topic (i.e. topic 351), of CRP and DCG curves. In order to facilitate the comprehension of the graph the bars showing the single contribution to the "cumulated" value of each document are also reported; the green color means exact positioning, the red color a position above the ideal, and the blue color a position below the ideal. This convention is also valid for DCG and its horizontal bar (i.e. the so-called ΔGain bar [13]): we use the color green for no gain, the blue color when a document is ranked below the ideal (we have a loss) and the red color when a document is ranked above the ideal (we have a gain). In this figure we can see that the distance between R and b_r gives us a visual measure of how much misplaced documents influence the initial part of the ranking list; the more relevant documents the system puts in high positions, the shorter the distance between R and b_r is. This fact is quantified by the ρ value; indeed, a high ρ value reflects a high number of relevant documents ranked in the expected position and a short distance between R and b_r. With respect to DCG, CRP allows for explicit considerations on the information value of late-ranked documents. After the b_r value, the CRP graph allows us to see in which positions misplaced documents are put and to which degree they contribute to the overall quality of the ranking. CRP increases by a step for every late-ranked document and the height of this step is proportional to the relevance of the document and to the position in which it lies.

Figure 3 shows the CRP Aggregate Graph for all the TREC 7 topics of the "bb1" run, by means of the Parallel Coordinates paradigm. It visualizes the four synthesis indicators of the CRP curve plus two parameters which characterize

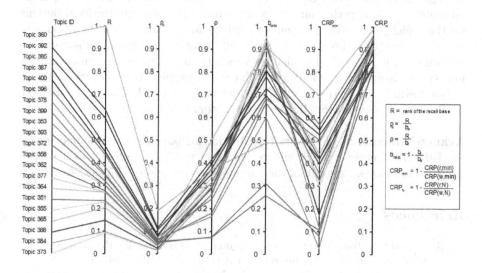

Fig. 3. CRP Parallel Coordinates Graph for the considered run (bb1 of TREC7)

the topic under investigation: R which is the recall base and $\rho_w = \frac{R}{b_w}$ which is the recovery value for the worst-case.

All the values are in the $[0,1]$ interval and a different color set is used to distinguish in a better way between the curves. This visualization allows us to see the correlation between the topics. We can point out the topic in which the run performs poorly (e.g. topic 393) and the topic for which it works fine (e.g. topic 394). The topics are ordered by their recall base in order to present a better overall visualization of the results.

5   Conclusions

In the present paper, we have proposed a new evaluation metric for Information Retrieval, the *Cumulated Relative Position (CRP)*. We started with the observation that a document of a given degree of relevance may be ranked too early or too late regarding the ideal ranking of documents for a query. Its relative position may therefore be negative, indicating too early ranking, zero indicating correct ranking, or positive, indicating too late ranking. By cumulating these relative rankings we indicate the net effect of document displacements, the CRP. We defined the CRP, and discussed its properties, formally. We also presented visualizations of the CRP that help analyze individual query performance, aggregate query performance, and compare the CRP performance with other IR metrics such as the DCG.

The CRP metric differs from prior standard IR metrics in explicitly handling document ranking misplacements either too early or too late given their degree of relevance and the ideal ranking. We believe that the CRP offers several advantages in IR evaluation because (a) it is obvious to interpret and it gives an estimate of ranking performance as a single measure relative to the ideal ranking for the topic; (b) it is independent on outliers since it focuses on the ranking of the result list; (c) it directly reports the effort wasted in examining suboptimal rankings; (d) it is based on graded relevance; (e) it can easily be summarized by four synthesis indicators; (f) it works fine with graphical representations.

Good evaluation metrics are required for progress in IR. We believe that the CRP metric is a useful tool in the IR evaluators tool box.

Acknowledgements. The work reported in this paper has been supported by the PROMISE network of excellence (contract n. 258191) project as a part of the 7th Framework Program of the European commission (FP7/2007-2013).

References

1. Sanderson, M.: Test Collection Based Evaluation of Information Retrieval Systems. Foundations and Trends in Information Retrieval (FnTIR) 4, 247–375 (2010)
2. Harman, D.K.: Information Retrieval Evaluation. Morgan & Claypool Publishers, USA (2011)

3. Kekäläinen, J., Järvelin, K.: Using Graded Relevance Assessments in IR Evaluation. Journal of the American Society for Information Science and Technology (JASIST) 53, 1120–1129 (2002)

4. Robertson, S.E., Kanoulas, E., Yilmaz, E.: Extending Average Precision to Graded Relevance Judgments. In: Proc. 33rd Annual International ACM SIGIR Conference on Research and Development in Information Retrieval (SIGIR 2010), pp. 603–610. ACM Press, New York (2010)

5. Järvelin, K., Kekäläinen, J.: Cumulated Gain-Based Evaluation of IR Techniques. ACM Transactions on Information Systems (TOIS) 20, 422–446 (2002)

6. Keskustalo, H., Järvelin, K., Pirkola, A., Kekäläinen, J.: Intuition-Supporting Visualization of User's Performance Based on Explicit Negative Higher-Order Relevance. In: Proc. 31st Annual International ACM SIGIR Conference on Research and Development in Information Retrieval (SIGIR 2008), pp. 675–681. ACM Press, New York (2008)

7. Korfhage, R.R.: Information Storage and Retrieval. Wiley Computer Publishing, John Wiley & Sons, Inc., USA (1997)

8. Salton, G., McGill, M.J.: Introduction to Modern Information Retrieval. McGraw-Hill, New York (1983)

9. Voorhees, E.M.: TREC: Continuing Information Retrieval's Tradition of Experimentation. Communications of the ACM (CACM) 50, 51–54 (2007)

10. Cosijn, E., Ingwersen, P.: Dimensions of Relevance. Information Processing & Management 36, 533–550 (2000)

11. Saracevic, T.: Relevance reconsidered. In: Ingwersen, P., Pors, N.O. (eds.) Proc. 2nd International Conference on Conceptions of Library and Information Science – Integration in Perspective (CoLIS 2), pp. 201–218. Royal School of Librarianship, Copenhagen (1996)

12. Sormunen, E.: Liberal Relevance Criteria of TREC: Counting on Negligible Documents? In: Proc. of the 25th International ACM SIGIR Conference on Research and Development in Information Retrieval, pp. 324–330. ACM Press (2002)

13. Ferro, N., Sabetta, A., Santucci, G., Tino, G.: Visual Comparison of Ranked Result Cumulated Gains. In: Proc. 2nd International Workshop on Visual Analytics (EuroVA 2011), pp. 21–24. Eurographics Association, Goslar (2011)

14. Voorhees, E., Harman, D.: Overview of the Seventh Text REtrieval Conference (TREC-7). In: NIST Special Publication 500-242: The Seventh Text REtrieval Conference (TREC 7). Springer, Heidelberg (1999)

Better than Their Reputation? On the Reliability of Relevance Assessments with Students

Philipp Schaer

GESIS – Leibniz Institute for the Social Sciences,
Unter Sachsenhausen 6-8, 50667 Cologne, Germany
philipp.schaer@gesis.org

Abstract. During the last three years we conducted several information retrieval evaluation series with more than 180 LIS students who made relevance
assessments on the outcomes of three specific retrieval services. In this study
we do not focus on the retrieval performance of our system but on the relevance
assessments and the inter-assessor reliability. To quantify the agreement we apply Fleiss' Kappa and Krippendorff's Alpha. When we compare these two statistical measures on average Kappa values were 0.37 and Alpha values 0.15.
We use the two agreement measures to drop too unreliable assessments from
our data set. When computing the differences between the unfiltered and the filtered data set we see a root mean square error between 0.02 and 0.12. We see
this as a clear indicator that disagreement affects the reliability of retrieval
evaluations. We suggest not to work with unfiltered results or to clearly document the disagreement rates.

Keywords: Evaluation, Students, Relevance Assessment, Information Retrieval, Inter-assessor Agreement, Inter-rater Agreement, Fleiss' Kappa, Krippendorff's Alpha.

1   Introduction

During the last three years we conducted several information retrieval evaluation series
regarding different retrieval-supporting services. More than 180 LIS students made
relevance assessments on the outcomes of three specific retrieval services. These three
services were designed to compensate typical problems that arise in metadata-driven
digital libraries, which are not adequately handled by a simple TF*IDF based retrieval.
The services are: a co-word analysis based query expansion mechanism and re-ranking
via Bradfordizing and Author Centrality. The overall system and the value added services, outlined in section 3.1, are well documented and previous evaluation results were
presented at conferences and journals before [14, 15, 18].

   While we did a study on the inter-assessor or inter-rater agreement for the first year
of our evaluation, until now we did no meta-analysis regarding the time period of
three years or the effects of the large number of students. Therefore the questions for
this work are: (1) How good and reliable are the relevance assessments of our students? (2) Can the quality and reliability be safely quantified? What methods should

T. Catarci et al. (Eds.): CLEF 2012, LNCS 7488, pp. 124–135, 2012.
© Springer-Verlag Berlin Heidelberg 2012

be used to quantify the reliability? (3) What effects would a data cleaning step bring up? Should we drop too unreliable assessments? Finally and more generally speaking we are interested in the question: What about the bad reputation of relevance assessment studies done with students or laymen?

The actual retrieval performance of the three value-added services and the pros and cons of each system is not the focus of this work. The services and their evaluation are a general framework for our studies on the inter-assessor reliability. In this paper we will analyse the quality of the assessments, measured in inter-assessor agreement by Fleiss' Kappa and Krippendorff's Alpha. While the first one is a standard measure recommended in Information Retrieval textbooks like Manning et al. [13], the second is rarely used in the IR and relevance assessment domain.

The paper is outlined as follows: We start with an overview on related work in the field of relevance assessment and the measurement of inter-assessor reliability in section 2. In section 3 we give a very short introduction of the three evaluated services, their implementation, materials and methods and the conducted relevance assessments. The results of our analysis are presented in section 4. We will close with a discussion and a look on future work in section 5.

2   Related Work

Information Retrieval (IR) test collections are typically built from a given set of documents, a set of topics and relevance judgments for documents that were made by a group of human assessors. The judgments are sometimes called assessments or ratings and therefore the people doing the judgments are called judges, assessors or raters. In this paper we will use the terms relevance assessments, assessors and inter-rater agreement respectively.

Since the early days of IR research and the construction of IR test collections a critical and general issue in conducting relevance assessment with more than one assessor per topic is the disagreement between the assessors. To get a feeling for the degree of agreement between the different assessors simple percentage-agreement or overlap counts were used in early TREC studies as documented by Voorhees [21], later Jaccard's coefficient (intersection/union) was used.

A variety of studies was compiled by Bailey et al. [4]. In their work they give a comprehensive overview on historical and recent studies on inter-assessor agreement and report on some characteristics of empirical studies of inter-assessor agreement in IR evaluation settings. We see a wide range of different settings from the number of relevance levels, number of topics, ratio of documents per topic, ratio of assessors per topic, to the kind of agreement measures that were reported in the original studies. For a short summary see table 1 which was compiled from the original paper from Bailey to allow a direct comparison to this study. In early years inter-assessor agreement measures like Jaccard coefficient or the intersection method were – and still today [16] are – used. These measures are getting unstable and unreliable as the number of categories or assessors increases. Later Kappa values from Cohen or Fleiss were used.

Fleiss' Kappa is a measure of inter-grader reliability or agreement for nominal or binary ratings and an extended version of Cohen's Kappa. While Cohen's Kappa is only suitable for two assessors, Fleiss' Kappa can be used for more than two assessors [7]. The computed Kappa values can be interpreted as the extent to which the observed amount of agreement among assessors exceeds what would be expected if all assessors made their ratings completely randomly. Kappa scores can range from -1 (no agreement) to 1 (full agreement). Landis and Koch [12] suggest interpreting the score as followed: $\kappa \leq 0$ = poor agreement, $0 \leq \kappa \leq 0.2$ = slight agreement, $0.2 \leq \kappa < 0.4$ = fair agreement, $0.4 \leq \kappa < 0.6$ = moderate agreement, $0.6 \leq \kappa < 0.8$ = substantial agreement, $0.8 \leq \kappa \leq 1$ = (almost) perfect agreement. These interpretations are not generally accepted and other interpretations are possible. Greve and Wentura [9] suggest interpreting scores $\kappa < .4$ as "not be taken too seriously" and values of $0.4 \leq \kappa < 0.6$ as acceptable. $0.75 \leq \kappa$ seems good up to excellent.

Besides Kappa some authors suggest to use Krippendorff's Alpha coefficient to measure agreement. While the use of Fleiss' and Cohen's Kappa is suggested in IR standard literature [13] and common practice in current research [2] Alpha coefficients are rather uncommon but are used in domains like opinion retrieval [5] or computational linguistics [3].

While for Kappa all assessors have to rate the same number of subjects and use the same scale the Alpha coefficient can usually handle more variations and computes reliabilities that are comparable across any numbers of assessors and values, different metrics, and unequal sample sizes. Krippendorff [11] argues for the use of Alpha in favour of other measure like Kappa because of its independence to the number of assessors and its robustness against imperfect data. For Krippendorff's Alpha there are the same doubts against such fixed and recommended values. Besides that Krippendorff himself pointed out that Alpha values are usually smaller than Kappa and that "except for perfect agreement, there are no magical numbers" [11]. Nevertheless he mentions $\alpha \geq 0.8$ as a threshold for perfect agreement.

Table 1. Overview on a compilation of studies (mainly taken from Bailey et al. [4] with additions from our own literature studies, marked by a citation) reporting characteristics of empirical studies of inter-assessor agreement.

researchers	relev. levels	topics	docs/ topic	ass./ topic	agreement + measure
Lesk & Salton	2	48	1268	2	31%, Jaccard
Cleverdon	5	32	200	4	-
Burgin	3	100	1239	4	40-55%, Jaccard
Voorhees & Harman	2	49	400	2	72%, overlay
Voorhees, Cormack	2+3	49	≈124	2-5	33%, Jaccard
Sormunen	4	38	31-200	2	custom
Trotman et al.	2	15	67-135	3-5	custom
Bailey et al. [4]	3	33	53-176	3	Cohen's κ
Piwowarski et al. [16]	2-4	20	-	2	23-31%, Jaccard
Schaer (this study)	2	10	40-50	2-13	Fleiss' κ and Krippendorff's α

3   Materials and Methods

During the last years we conducted several relevance assessment evaluation series using three different retrieval services. The evaluation was done three times during the winter terms at University of Applied Sciences, Darmstadt and two times at Humboldt University, Berlin respectively.

3.1   Evaluated Services

Standard IR methods like TF*IDF are text-centric, which means they propose a text-based relevance ranking: These methods assign a weight to term t in document d which is influenced by different occurrences of t and d. While in general these methods work rather well especially in special domains like digital libraries and domain specific databases problems like the "language problem" and the need for alternative rankings become clear. We developed three science-model-driven methods that try to overcome these retrieval issues:

(1) Search Term Recommenders (STR), which are an approach to compensate the long known language problem in Information Retrieval. STRs are based on statistical co-word analysis and build associations between query terms and controlled terms (i.e. from a thesaurus). The co-word analysis implies a semantic association between the uncontrolled and the controlled terms. In our setup we use STRs for automatic query expansion where the original query of the user is enhanced with "semantically near" terms from a controlled vocabulary.

(2) Bradfordizing is an alternative mechanism to re-rank result lists according to core journals to bypass the problem of very large and unstructured result sets. The approach of Bradfordizing is to use characteristic concentration effects (Bradford's law of scattering) that appear typically in journal literature. Documents in core journals – journals that publish frequently on a topic – are ranked higher than documents that were published in journals from the following zones.

(3) Author centrality is another way of re-ranking result sets. Here the concept of centrality in a network of authors is an additional approach for the problem of large and unstructured result sets. The intention behind this ranking model is to make use of knowledge about the interaction and cooperation behaviour in special fields of research. The model is based on a network analytical view and differs greatly from conventional text-oriented ranking methods like TF*IDF.

3.2   Evaluation Setup

In our setup we used the SOLIS database with approx. 370.000 single documents from the social science domain. The database largely consists of metadata on scientific literature and is a superset of the GIRT corpus used in the TREC and CLEF evaluation campaigns. We only used a subset of the available metadata so that the assessed documents included title, abstract, author names and controlled keywords. We intentionally left out information like the publication year, publishers or the journal the documents were published in since we want our assessors to solely rely on the actual content information not additional hints that might let them draw conclusions from the currency or the reputation of a journal or publisher. The assessment system, which was built on top of the IRSA toolkit[1] and all documents were in German. All written examples in this paper are translated.

In our assessment each participants had to complete and assess one concrete search task, which was taken from the CLEF campaign. After a briefing each student had to choose one out of ten different predefined topics (namely CLEF topics 83, 84, 88, 93, 96, 105, 110, 153, 166 and 173). Topic title and the description were presented to form the information need (see table 1). Since the assessors were no domain experts in the social science domain we choose these topics because of their broad connection to youth, media, education, Germany in general and their ability to be used as common-sense retrieval tasks.

Table 2. Ten topics taken from the CLEF campaign, which were used in the relevance assessments

Topic	Title	Description
83	Media and War	Find documents on the commentatorship of the press and other media from war regions.
84	New Media in Education	Find documents reporting on benefits and risks of using new technology such as computers or the Internet in schools.
88	Sports in Nazi Germany	Find documents about the role of sports in the German Third Reich.
93	Burnout Syndrome	Find documents reporting on the burnout syndrome.
96	Costs of Vocational Education	Find documents reporting on the costs and benefits of vocational education.
105	Graduates and Labour Market	Find documents reporting on the job market for university graduates.
110	Suicide of Young People	Find documents investigating suicides in teenagers and young adults.
153	Childlessness in Germany	Information on the factors for childlessness in Germany
166	Poverty in Germany	Research papers and publications on poverty and homelessness in Germany.
173	Propensity towards violence among youths	Find reports, cases, empirical studies and analyses on the capacity of adolescents for violence.

The assessors saw a pooled list of result documents, so the origin of each document was disguised. The pool was formed out of the top n=10 ranked documents from each service and the initial TF*IDF ranked result set from the Solr search engine, respec-

---

[1] http://sourceforge.net/projects/irsa/

tively. Duplicates were removed, so that the size of the sample pools in 2010 was between 34 and 39 documents each. In 2011 and 2012 we added a so-called random ranking service. This service just randomly takes 10 documents from the original Solr query, which resulted in slightly larger result sets in 2011 and 2012. The assessors could choose to judge relevant or not relevant (binary decision).

3.3 Participants

A total of n=188 undergrad library and information science students contributed to the evaluation. They did a total of 9,226 single document assessments. Because some of the assessors didn't judge all of the documents we had to filter out some of the assessments. After a data cleaning step n=168 students remain in the data set. We discarded all assessments with more than 5% error rates (e.g. more than 2 documents missing from a theoretical data pool of 40 documents). In 2010 we had a total of 75 students doing the assessments, in 2011 we had 57 and in 2012 36 students participated. As stated above the evaluation was done three times during the winter terms at University of Applied Sciences, Darmstadt and two times at Humboldt University, Berlin respectively.

3.4 Computing Inter-assessor Agreement

We briefly list the basic approaches to compute Fleiss' Kappa and Krippendorff's Alpha to get a feeling for the two computations. In general both methods try to compute the amount of agreement by defining agreement as

$$\text{Agreement} = 1 - \frac{D_o}{D_e} = 1 - \frac{\text{Observed Disagreement}}{\text{Expected Disagreement}}$$

but they differ in the way they operationalize these computations (for a more comprehensive description see [10]).

Given a generic two by two contingency table 3 with the proportions a, b, c and d, where a + d is the observed agreement and b + c is the disagreement. The proportion of 0s in the data is given by $\bar{p} = (p_A + p_B)/2$ and the proportion of 1s by $\bar{q} = (q_A + q_B)/2$ or $1 - \bar{p}$. n is the number of 0s and 1s used jointly.

Kappa and Alpha are now computed by:

$$\kappa = 1 - \frac{b+c}{p_A q_b + p_B q_A}$$

and

$$\alpha = 1 - \frac{b+c}{\frac{n}{n-1} 2\bar{p}\bar{q}}$$

Table 3. Two by two contingency table (taken from [11])

Assessor A

		0	1	
Assessor B	0	a	b	p_B
	1	c	d	q_B
		p_A	q_A	1

All listed Kappa and Alpha values were computed using the R statistics software [17] and the irr package [8] respectively.

4   Results

We report on the outcomes of the inter-assessor agreements and on the implications these agreements or disagreements have on the evaluation of the initially described retrieval services when we drop the unreliably assessments from our data set.

4.1   Inter-assessor Agreement

The results of the inter-assessor agreement tests are listed in table 4. They are grouped per year and average values are given in the last columns and the last line. We can see that the average number of assessors per topic is between 4 and 8.7, the average Kappa values are between 0.210 and 0.524. Alpha values are generally below the Kappa values and the average Alpha values are between -0.018 and 0.279. Kappa values are all in the region of "fair" to "moderate" agreement but the Alpha values are far away from being "acceptable". The general agreement rate is low.

When we apply a Pearson correlation we get a relatively weak correlation coefficient of 0.447 on the average values. The highest correlation on a per year basis is the on from 2010 with 0.581, the other correlation coefficient are 0.406 for 2011 and 0.326 for 2012. Nevertheless we can see some essential misinterpretation on a per topic/year basis. While topic 96 in the year 2012 had one of the highest Alpha values the corresponding Kappa values are nearly 0. The opposite is true for topic 83 from 2010: here one of the highest Kappa values of 0.535 only got an Alpha value of 0.12.

We can see large differences between the different topics and years but the differences are (1) connected to the number of students and (2) the specific topic. While in 2010 the number of student assessors per topic was 7.5 and the correlation between Kappa and Alpha was 0.581, in 2012 only 3.6 students per topic had a lower correlation coefficient. The same is true to specific topics. Topics 153 and 173 both got very low Alpha and Kappa values although they were judged by 5 students on average.

Table 4. Inter-assessor agreement measured with Fleiss' Kappa and Krippendorff's Alpha for the years 2010 – 2012 and the corresponding average over all three years. The number of assessors per topic is given by n.

	2010			2011			2012			Average		
Topic	n	α	κ	n	α	κ	n	α	κ	n	α	κ
83	13	.120	.535	8	.229	.412	5	.092	.318	8.7	.147	.421
84	9	.165	.283	5	.073	.480	3	.169	.366	5.7	.136	.376
88	6	.181	.528	3	.327	.257	5	.197	.550	4.7	.235	.445
93	10	.036	.330	5	.375	.713	3	.195	.529	6.0	.202	.524
96	2	.293	.591	9	.186	.113	4	.358	.001	5.0	.279	.235
105	4	.125	.536	4	.068	.345	4	.052	.307	4.0	.082	.396
110	5	.148	.223	8	.104	.386	4	.308	.413	5.7	.187	.341
153	9	-.003	.194	7	.012	.304	3	-.063	.132	6.3	-.018	.210
166	8	.100	.382	5	.274	.505	2	.236	.536	5.0	.203	.474
173	9	.076	.433	3	.000	.297	3	-.081	.084	5.0	-.002	.271
avg.	7.5	.124	.403	5.7	.165	.381	3.6	.146	.323	5.6	.145	.369

4.2   The Effects of Dropping Unreliable Assessments

Since the agreement rates measured by Kappa and Alpha reported in section 4.1 were below the recommended values for "acceptable" agreements we decided to measure the effects of data cleaning. Given the fact that there are no "magic numbers" we tried to pick thresholds that can be applied to the given data. If we had applied the high threshold reported in section 2 of κ, α ≥ 0.8 no single assessment would have remained in the data set.

In table 5 we see two different result sets containing the precision values (p@10) for the different services on a per topic basis. The first column set contains the unfiltered judgments from all assessors. Only the obviously wrong and sparse data sets were cleaned from this one (see section 3.3). The second column set contains the remaining results after all assessments with κ < 0.4 were removed from the result set. The same method is applied for the last column set where the threshold was α < 0.1.

Topics 153 (Childlessness in Germany) and 173 (Propensity towards violence among youths) contained the most inconsistencies. In all three years the Kappa and Alpha values were below the thresholds (only the Kappa values from 2010 were above the threshold). This way almost no assessments remained so that the two topics were mostly dropped for the Kappa-filter and completely dropped for the Alpha-filter. In total we had to drop 17 out of 30 assessment sets due to the Kappa filter and 11 due to the Alpha filter. For the Kappa filter no single topic had reliable assessments for all three years.

Table 5. Precision@10 values for five different retrieval services: SOLR (TF*IDF ranked, unprocessed baseline), RAND (the same baseline set but random ranking), AUTH (alternative ranking based on author centrality), BRAD (alternative ranking based on core journals, Bradfordizing) and STR (Query Expansion with controlled thesaurus terms). The left column set shows the unfiltered results from all assessors. The two right column sets are filtered with Fleiss Kappa and Krippendorff's Alpha, respectively. Empty cells are dropped values in all three years due to a too low inter-assessor agreement rate. The last line shows root mean square error between the unfiltered and filtered results.

Topic	Original, unfiltered results (o)					Filtered with Kappa > .4 (f_κ)					Filtered with Alpha > .1 (f_α)				
	SOLR	RAND	AUTH	BRAD	STR	SOLR	RAND	AUTH	BRAD	STR	SOLR	RAND	AUTH	BRAD	STR
83	.75	.39	.47	.27	.75	.74	.30	.43	.22	.74	.74	.30	.43	.22	.74
84	.77	.35	.32	.64	.57	.79	.31	.30	.65	.51	.80	.43	.30	.61	.54
88	.47	.45	.14	.66	.54	.47	.54	.16	.69	.49	.47	.42	.13	.66	.54
93	.68	.46	.68	.73	.57	.63	.44	.62	.71	.41	.63	.44	.62	.71	.41
96	.40	.45	.80	.59	.49	.40		.85	.70	.35	.41	.45	.82	.61	.47
105	.54	.46	.63	.51	.69	.67		.65	.59	.45	.67		.65	.59	.45
110	.66	.51	.71	.35	.84	.70	.45	.68	.30	.83	.68	.49	.71	.37	.85
153	.53	.36	.47	.51	.56										
166	.18	.46	.68	.55	.74	.23	.48	.70	.53	.84	.21	.48	.68	.54	.76
173	.47	.70	.63	.51	.58	.40		.58	.49	.74					
avg. prec.	.55	.46	.55	.53	.63	.56	.42	.55	.54	.60	.57	.43	.54	.54	.60
RMSerr(o,f)						.03	.05	.06	.05	.12	.02	.03	.05	.05	.10

To quantify the difference between the filtered and the unfiltered assessments sets and their values we applied the root mean square (RMS) error:

$$RMSerr(o,f) = \sqrt{\frac{1}{N}\sum_{i=1}^{N}(o_i - f_i)^2}$$

where o_i and f_i are the original/unfiltered and filtered values, respectively.

The RMSerr values are reported on the last line. We see moderate but considerable error rates between the unfiltered and filtered results. For the services SOLR, RAND, AUTH and BRAD the values are roughly around 0.05 for the Kappa-filtered and a little lower for the Alpha-filtered. The STR error values are 0.10 for the Kappa-filtered and 0.12 for the Alpha-filtered.

5   Discussion and Conclusion

When we look at the general agreement rate of our assessors we see a rather large range of results. In general and on average the agreement rates are fair to moderate but far away from being substantial or even perfect. On first sight the bad reputation of students doing relevance assessments seems legitimate: In the terms of Bailey et al. we were using "bronze standard judges" – so a perfect agreement could not be expected. On the other hand we see large differences between the different years and topics. Although we only had a small number of 10 topics in this study (which is quite small compared to the usual 25 – 50 topics suggested [20]) we had a high number of 5.6 assessors per topic. Since we saw that generally Kappa values are more prone to different numbers of assessors and does not scale that well compared to Alpha values we argue that beside the general practice of computing percentage overlaps, Jaccard coefficients and Fleiss' Kappa other values like Krippendorff's Alpha should be considered to get a more precise quantification of the agreement of the assessors and therefore a hint on the reliability of the collected assessment data.

Is there a general rule of thumb on how many assessors per query are necessary? Ideally, a large number of assessors per query should be used in an assessment. Recent approaches of using crowd-sourcing methods like Amazon's Mechanical Turk to do large-scale evaluations without domain experts are exactly going into that direction. But in the light of the rather low inter-assessor agreement rates in this controlled evaluation setup the uncontrolled situations in the crowd-sourcing approaches are debateable. So far and to our knowledge no Kappa or Alpha studies were done in this area yet. Studies by Alonso et al. [1] only reported on Jaccard coefficient and overlap counts.

What are good topics for lay assessors like students? Are their "easy" or "hard" topics in our assessment? Given the multidimensionality of relevance and the various relevance criteria users employ to judge the relevance, like described by Borlund [6], we should further analyse the observed disagreements and the connection to certain topics. We actually know very few on the motivation and the reasons for the disagreements in our assessment scenario.

When we apply the computed agreement rates to locate and filter out disputable assessment sets we see clear effects on the measured retrieval performance. In some cases this effect is quite drastic – like the different performance rates of the STR. This is in line with the general understanding of inter-assessor studies in other domains: "Reliability is [...] a prerequisite for demonstrating the validity of the coding scheme – that is, to show that the coding scheme captures the 'truth' of the phenomenon being studied" [3]. But by computing the agreement or disagreement of assessors we can only draw conclusions on the *stability* and *reproducibility* of our data, not inevitably the *accuracy* of our results. To compute the last we would need a gold standard, which does not exist in our setting.

We see the effects of our filtering as a clear indicator that disagreement affects the reliability of evaluations. However "no consistent conclusion on how disagreement affects the reliability of evaluation has yet been drawn" [19] in the IR community. We should be carful drawing conclusions from unfiltered results (like "The STR approach clearly outperforms the other retrieval services."). We therefore suggest not to work with unfiltered results or – since thresholds are always debateable and can be interchanged to higher or lower values – to clearly document the immanent differences and disagreements between the assessors. The differences should be presented in the results using standard measures of inter-assessor agreement like Cohen's/Fleiss' Kappa or Krippendorff's Alpha. This way we would make a huge step towards more sound evaluation data sets.

Acknowledgements. We would like to thank Philipp Mayr (University of Applied Sciences, Darmstadt) and Vivien Petras (Humboldt University, Berlin) who supervised the students during the winter semesters of 2010-2012 and Hasan Bas and Peter Mutschke who developed the assessment component and the Author Centrality library respectively that were used in the evaluation systems. This work was partly funded by DFG (grant no. SU 647/5-2).

References

1. Alonso, O., Schenkel, R., Theobald, M.: Crowdsourcing Assessments for XML Ranked Retrieval. In: Gurrin, C., He, Y., Kazai, G., Kruschwitz, U., Little, S., Roelleke, T., Rüger, S., van Rijsbergen, K. (eds.) ECIR 2010. LNCS, vol. 5993, pp. 602–606. Springer, Heidelberg (2010)
2. Arguello, J., Diaz, F., Callan, J., Carterette, B.: A Methodology for Evaluating Aggregated Search Results. In: Clough, P., Foley, C., Gurrin, C., Jones, G.J.F., Kraaij, W., Lee, H., Mudoch, V. (eds.) ECIR 2011. LNCS, vol. 6611, pp. 141–152. Springer, Heidelberg (2011)
3. Artstein, R., Poesio, M.: Inter-coder agreement for computational linguistics. Comput. Linguist. 34(4), 555–596 (2008)
4. Bailey, P., Craswell, N., Soboroff, I., Thomas, P., de Vries, A.P., Yilmaz, E.: Relevance assessment: are judges exchangeable and does it matter. In: Proceedings of the 31st Annual International ACM SIGIR Conference on Research and Development in Information Retrieval, pp. 667–674. ACM, New York (2008)
5. Bermingham, A., Smeaton, A.F.: A study of inter-annotator agreement for opinion retrieval. In: Proceedings of the 32nd International ACM SIGIR Conference on Research and Development in Information Retrieval, pp. 784–785. ACM, New York (2009)
6. Borlund, P.: The concept of relevance in IR. Journal of the American Society for Information Science and Technology 54(10), 913–925 (2003)
7. Fleiss, J.L.: Measuring nominal scale agreement among many raters. Psychological Bulletin 76(5), 378–382 (1971)
8. Gamer, M., Lemon, J., Puspendra Singh, I.F.: irr: Various Coefficients of Interrater Reliability and Agreement (2010)
9. Greve, W., Wentura, D.: Wissenschaftliche Beobachtung: eine Einführung. Beltz, PsychologieVerlagsUnion, Weinheim (1997)
10. Krippendorff, K.: Computing Krippendorff's Alpha-Reliability (2011), http://repository.upenn.edu/asc_papers/43
11. Krippendorff, K.: Reliability in Content Analysis: Some Common Misconceptions and Recommendations. Human Communication Research 30(3), 411–433 (2004)

12. Landis, J.R., Koch, G.G.: The measurement of observer agreement for categorical data. Biometrics 33(1), 159–174 (1977)
13. Manning, C.D., Raghavan, P., Schütze, H.: Introduction to Information Retrieval. Cambridge University Press, Cambridge (2008)
14. Mayr, P., Mutschke, P., Petras, V., Schaer, P., Sure, Y.: Applying Science Models for Search. In: 12. Internationales Symposium für Informationswissenschaft (ISI) (2011)
15. Mutschke, P., Mayr, P., Schaer, P., Sure, Y.: Science models as value-added services for scholarly information systems. Scientometrics 89(1), 349–364 (2011)
16. Piwowarski, B., Trotman, A., Lalmas, M.: Sound and complete relevance assessment for XML retrieval. ACM Trans. Inf. Syst. 27(1), 1:1–1:37 (2008)
17. R Development Core Team: R: A Language and Environment for Statistical Computing, Vienna, Austria (2011).
18. Schaer, P., Mayr, P., Mutschke, P.: Implications of Inter-Rater Agreement on a Student Information Retrieval Evaluation. In: Atzmüller, M., Benz, D., Hotho, A., Stumme, G. (eds.) Proceedings of LWA 2010 Workshop-Woche: Lernen, Wissen & Adaptivitaet, Kassel, Germany (2010)
19. Song, R., Guo, Q., Zhang, R., Xin, G., Wen, J.-R., Yu, Y., Hon, H.-W.: Select-the-Best-Ones: A new way to judge relative relevance. Inf. Process. Manage. 47(1), 37–52 (2011)
20. Voorhees, E.M.: Topic set size redux. In: Proceedings of the 32nd International ACM SIGIR Conference on Research and Development in Information Retrieval, pp. 806–807. ACM, New York (2009)
21. Voorhees, E.M.: Variations in relevance judgments and the measurement of retrieval effectiveness. Inf. Process. Manage. 36(5), 697–716 (2000)

Comparing IR System Components Using Beanplots

Jens Kürsten and Maximilian Eibl

Chemnitz University of Technology, Dept. of Computer Science, Chemnitz, Germany
{jens.kuersten,eibl}@informatik.tu-chemnitz.de

Abstract. In this poster we demonstrate an approach to gain a better understanding of the interactions between search tasks, test collections and components and configurations of retrieval systems by testing a large set of experiment configurations against standard ad-hoc test collections.

Keywords: Ad-hoc Retrieval, Component-based Evaluation.

1 Motivation

This article addresses a key problem of system-driven evaluation tasks and the increased complexity of IR systems: ranking modern IR systems according to a suitable effectiveness metric for a search task and its underlying document collection has only little value, if the information on the relations between the systems and their configuration remains shallow or unknown.

In order to overcome this limitation it has been proposed put the emphasis of the evaluation on the key components like text transformation [1] or automatic query expansion [2]. A general review of component-level architectures for evaluation is given in [3]. The main focus of this work lies in the combined analysis of different IR system component implementations that includes stemming, ranking, and automatic feedback algorithms. This approach is based on the idea that search tasks, test collections, and system components result in interactions that need to be studied in more detail in order to be able to separate system- and component-based effects.

The presented experiments were conducted using the Xtrieval framework [4], which provides seamless access to underlying IR libraries and toolkits like Apache Lucene, Terrier, and Lemur.

2 Component-Level Comparison of System Configurations

The goal of component-level evaluation is to provide an understanding of how one implementation of a particular system component relates to others. The approach to compare individual component instances that is used here is called beanplot visualisation [5]. It allows a visual comparison of the distribution of repeated measures. Three stemmers, ten ranking algorithms, and a set of 183 automatic feedback configurations were used to simulate experiments from different participants of a specific IR task.

Fig. 1 shows the beanplots for the resulting 5,490 individual system configurations tested against the TREC45-CR collection. The ranking model is treated as variable

T. Catarci et al. (Eds.): CLEF 2012, LNCS 7488, pp. 136–137, 2012.

factor, i.e. each of the ten "beans" shows the distribution of the MAP values for the same set of 549 configurations. The resulting shapes for TF-IDF, BM25 and DLH13 in Fig. 1 follow a normal distribution. In contrast to that, the curve for Lucene appears to be a mixture of a normal and a uniform distribution. The curve for IFB2 can be interpreted as a bi-modal distribution. A normal distribution indicates that the ranking model is not affected by other components of the system configuration. Bimodal or multimodal distributions designate that some other part of the system configuration affects MAP considerably, most likely even more than the ranking model in question. As a result, these models need to be tuned with respect to the entire IR system configuration to obtain optimal results in terms of retrieval effectiveness. The number of peaks in bi- or multi-modal distributions provides a direction for further analysis.

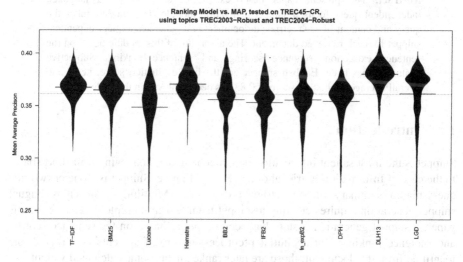

Fig. 1. Beanplot visualisation that shows the MAP distribution of 5,490 system configurations (by altering the ranking model in each of the beans) for the TREC45-CR collection.

References

1. Ferro, N., Harman, D.: CLEF 2009: Grid@CLEF Pilot Track Overview. In: Peters, C., Di Nunzio, G.M., Kurimo, M., Mandl, T., Mostefa, D., Peñas, A., Roda, G. (eds.) CLEF 2009. LNCS, vol. 6241, pp. 552–565. Springer, Heidelberg (2010)
2. Harman, D., Buckley, C.: Overview of the Reliable Information Access Workshop. Information Retrieval 12(6), 615–641 (2009)
3. Hanbury, A., Müller, H.: Automated Component–Level Evaluation: Present and Future. In: Agosti, M., Ferro, N., Peters, C., de Rijke, M., Smeaton, A. (eds.) CLEF 2010. LNCS, vol. 6360, pp. 124–135. Springer, Heidelberg (2010)
4. Kürsten, J., Wilhelm, T., Eibl, M.: Extensible Retrieval and Evaluation Framework: Xtrieval. In: Baumeister, J., Atzmüller, M. (eds.) LWA 2008, University of Würzburg, pp. 107–110 (2008)
5. Kampstra, P.: Beanplot: A Boxplot Alternative for Visual Comparison of Distributions. Journal of Statistical Software 28(1), 1–9 (2008)

Language Independent
Query Focused Snippet Generation

Pinaki Bhaskar and Sivaji Bandyopadhyay

Dept. of Computer Science & Engineering, Jadavpur University, Kolkata, India
pinaki.bhaskar@gmail.com, sivaji_cse_ju@yahoo.com

Abstract. The present paper describes the development of a language independent query focused snippet generation module. This module takes the query and content of each retrieved document and generates a query dependent snippet for each retrieved document. The algorithm of this module based on the sentence extraction, sentence scoring and sentence ranking. Subjective evaluation has been. English snippet got the best evaluation score, i.e. 1 and overall average evaluation score of 0.83 has been achieved in the scale of 0 to 1.

1   Introduction

Snippet is the most salient information in a document and conveying it in short space. In the case of Information Retrieval or any Search Engine, Snippet is a one or two line query-biased summary of the retrieved document. Multilingual or cross lingual snippet generation requires creating a snippet from text in multiple languages. In this paper, a snippet generation system has been proposed based on the sentence scoring and sentence ranking. During initial preprocessing, text fragments are filtered and identified from the document; those are later ranked using some calculated weight.

2   Key Term Extraction

First the query is parsed while the Multiword Word Expressions (MWE) and Named Entities (NE) are identified and stop words are removed. Now the query terms are stemmed and extracted with their Boolean relations (AND or OR). Like the query terms extraction, the title words and meta keywords are also extracted form the title and meta information of the retrieved document.

3   Top Sentence Identification

Documents are parsed and all the extracted sentences are now searched for query terms, title words and meta keywords. Extracted sentences are given some weight according to search and ranked on the basis of the calculated weight using equation 1.

T. Catarci et al. (Eds.): CLEF 2012, LNCS 7488, pp. 138–140, 2012.

$$W = \sum_{t=0}^{n_t} (n_t - t + 1) \left(\sum_p \left(1 - \frac{f_p^t - 1}{N_s} \right) \right) \times b \qquad (1)$$

where, W is the term dependent score of the sentence s, t is the no. of the term, n_t is the total no. of term, f_p^t is the possession of the word which was matched with the term t in the sentence s, N_s is the total no. of words in sentence s and b is boost factor of the term, which is 3, 2 or 1 for query terms, title words and meta keywords respectively. After calculating three scores for three types of term, the final weight of each sentence is calculated by simply adding all the three scores.

After weight calculating, sentences are sorted in descending order of their weight. Now, top three ranked sentences are taken for the Snippet Generation. If all these three sentences are small enough to fit into the snippet without trimming themselves and overflowing the maximum length of a snippet, then after this module the system goes directly to the Snippet Generation module to generate the snippet of the document. Otherwise it goes through the Snippet Unit Selection module.

4   Snippet Unit Selection

If the total length of the top three ranked sentences of the document is larger than the maximum length of a snippet, then all these three sentences are split into snippet units. Snippet unit is basically a phrase or clause of a sentence. The snippet units are extracted in this module using the syntactic information like brackets, semi colon (';'), coma (',') etc. available in the sentences.

Weights of all the extracted snippet units have to be calculated to identify most relevant and most important snippet units. The same Weight assigning module using equation 1 is used to calculate the weights of snippet units too. After calculating weights of all the snippet units, they are sorted in descending order of their weight in the same way of Sentence Ranking module.

5   Snippet Generation

This is the final and most critical module of this system. This module generates the Snippet from the sorted snippet units. As [7] using equation 2, the module selects the ranked snippet units subject to maximum length of the snippet has been reached.

$$\sum_i l_i S_i < L \qquad (2)$$

where l_i is the length of snippet unit i, S_i is a binary variable representing the selection of snippet unit i and L (=100 words) is the maximum length of the snippet.

Now, the selected snippet units are reordered according to their order of appearance in the text. If two consecutive snippet units are selected then they are concatenated without an ellipsis other wise two snippet units are concatenated with ellipsis. All the query words in the snippet are then highlighted by the html tag.

6   Evaluation

Subjective evaluation has been done to evaluate the generated snippet. Total 22 evaluators in 7 different languages have given a score between 0 to 1 as per how much he/she satisfied with generated snippet. The evaluation scores for all the seven languages have been shown in the figure 1.

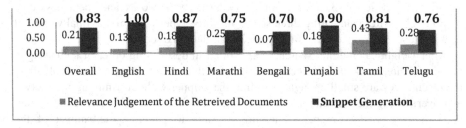

Fig. 1. Chart showing the evaluation scores of Ranking and Snippet Generation for each language

Acknowledgments. The work has been carried out with support from Department of Information Technology (DIT), Govt. of India funded Project Development of "Cross Lingual Information Access (CLIA)" System Phase II.

References

1. Huang, Y., Liu, Z., Chen, Y.: Query Biased Snippet Generation in XML Search. In: SIGMOD 2008, Vancouver, BC, Canada (2008)
2. Radev, D.R., Jing, H., Styś, M., Tam, D.: Centroid- based summarization of multiple documents. Information Processing and Management 40, 919–938 (2004)
3. Lin, C.-Y., Hovy, E.H.: From Single to Multidocument Summarization: A Prototype System and its Evaluation, pp. 457–464. ACL (2002)
4. Zhang, Y., Ji, X., Chu, C.H., Zha, H.: Correlating Summarization of Multisource News with KWay Graph Biclustering. SIGKDD Explorations 6(2), 34–42 (2004); Association for Computing Machinery: Computing Reviews 24(11), 503–512 (1983)
5. Varadarajan, R., Hristidis, V.: A system for query specific document summarization. In: CIKM, pp. 622–631 (2006)
6. Paladhi, S., Bandyopadhyay, S.: A Document Graph Based Query Focused Multi-Document Summarizer. In: The 2nd International Workshop on Cross Lingual Information Access (CLIA), pp. 55–62 (2008)
7. Bhaskar, P., Bandyopadhyay, S.: A Query Focused Multi Document Automatic Summarization. In: The 24th Pacific Asia Conference on Language, Information and Computation (PACLIC 24), Tohoku University, Sendai, Japan (2010)
8. Bhaskar, P., Bandyopadhyay, S.: A Query Focused Automatic Multi Document Summarizer. In: The International Conference on Natural Language Processing (ICON), IIT, Kharagpur, India (2010)
9. Turpin, A., Tsegay, Y., Hawking, D., Williams, H.E.: Fast Generation of Result Snippets in Web Search. In: SIGIR (2007)

A Test Collection to Evaluate Plagiarism by Missing or Incorrect References

Solange de L. Pertile and Viviane P. Moreira

Instituto de Informática, UFRGS, Brazil
{slpertile,viviane}@inf.ufrgs.br

Abstract. In recent years, several methods and tools been developed together with test collections to aid in plagiarism detection. However, both methods and collections have focused on content analysis, overlooking citation analysis. In this paper, we aim at filling this gap and present a test collection with cases of plagiarism by missing and incorrect references. The collection contains automatically generated academic papers in which passages from other documents have been inserted. Such passages were either: adequately referenced (i.e., not plagiarized), not referenced, or incorrectly referenced. Annotation files identifying each passage enable the evaluation of plagiarism detection systems.

1 Introduction

Plagiarism is one of the most serious forms of academic misconduct. It consists in the act of presenting any type of work without crediting the rightful authors. Due to the enormous number of documents available in digital format, accessing information is becoming easier, which in turn facilitates its copy and distribution and makes it impossible to manually check for illegal copies of this information. Thus, current technologies are still seeking an efficient and effective way to protect intellectual property and at the same time, provide access to those who need the information [1].

Different detection strategies have been proposed to deal with the various forms of plagiarism. In order to evaluate such strategies, test collections become necessary. These collections are typically composed of a corpus and a set of annotations which will enable the evaluation of the quality of each detection method. Existing test collections are devoted to identifying similarity of content [2,3,4]. However, to be able to distinguish between a plagiarized passage and a passage that was extracted from a source which has been referenced, citation analysis is needed. In this paper we report on the creation of PlaMIR – a test collection with cases of plagiarism by missing or incorrect reference. To the best of our knowledge, this is the first test collection for this type of plagiarism.

2 Creating the Collection

The strategy used to create the collection was to generate artificial documents (i.e., academic papers) and insert into them passages from other papers which

T. Catarci et al. (Eds.): CLEF 2012, LNCS 7488, pp. 141–143, 2012.

are either plagiarized or non-plagiarized. The PlaMIR test collection is composed of four parts: (i) a corpus with 963 source documents; (ii) bibliographic records for the source documents; (iii) a corpus of 1000 suspicious documents; and (iv) annotation files describing where the passages were inserted and whether they are considered plagiarism. Note that we cannot distribute the source documents since they are real research papers protected by copyright. However, to make the collection usable, we provide links to them. PlaMIR is available for download from: http://www.inf.ufrgs.br/~slpertile/plamir.html.

Generating Suspicious Documents: The first step was to generate 1000 papers in the area of Computer Science using the SCIgen [5] tool. We will refer to those as *suspicious documents*.

Obtaining Source Documents: To obtain *source documents*, from which the passages were going to be taken, we collected PDF versions for 963 research papers, together with their bibliographic records, from DBLP [6].

Inserting Passages in the Suspicious Documents: Once the corpora of suspicious and source documents are obtained, we simulate artificial plagiarism cases in the suspicious documents. The source documents used to extract artificial plagiarized and non-plagiarized passages were randomly selected. Each suspicious document may have passages from up to 10 source documents. From each source document, we randomly picked a number of passages to insert in the suspicious documents. A suspicious document can simultaneously receive non-plagiarized and plagiarized passages. 946 suspicious documents received non-plagiarized passages and 818 suspicious documents received plagiarized passages. For each passage, we randomly chose whether it would be a non-plagiarism case, a case of plagiarism by missing reference, or a case of plagiarism by incorrect reference. The length of the passage, the source document that it was taken from and the position where it was inserted in the suspicious document are crucial to evaluate the detection systems. Thus, they are recorded in the annotation file. When the passage is not plagiarized, the corresponding bibliographic reference for the source document is inserted into the reference block of the suspicious document. In cases of plagiarism by incorrect reference, the passage receives information that allows us to uniquely identify the reference for the source document. In these cases, the reference included in the reference block is extracted from another source document, not corresponding to the one cited in the passage.

3   Conclusion

In this paper, we discussed the creation of a test collection designed to assist in the evaluation of systems for the automatic detection of plagiarism by missing or incorrect reference. The PlaMIR collection has artificial documents in which we inserted passages taken from other documents. These passages were either plagiarism by missing reference, by incorrect reference, or they had the appropriate reference, making them non-plagiarism cases. Future work will include the application of paraphrasing techniques to disguise the plagiarism cases.

Acknowledgements. This work was partially funded by CNPq (project no. 479703/2010-8). Solange Pertile is funded by a CAPES scholarship.

References

1. Brin, S., Davis, J., Garcia-Molina, H.: Copy detection mechanisms for digital documents. In: SIGMOD, pp. 398–409 (1995)
2. PAN: Uncovering plagiarism, authorship, and social software misuse, http://pan.webis.de/ (accessed April 04, 2012)
3. CL!TR: Cross-language !ndian text reuse, http://users.dsic.upv.es/grupos/nle/fire-workshop-clitr.html (accessed June 21, 2012)
4. Corezola Pereira, R., Moreira, V.P., Galante, R.: A New Approach for Cross-Language Plagiarism Analysis. In: Agosti, M., Ferro, N., Peters, C., de Rijke, M., Smeaton, A. (eds.) CLEF 2010. LNCS, vol. 6360, pp. 15–26. Springer, Heidelberg (2010)
5. SCIgen: An automatic CS paper generator, http://pdos.csail.mit.edu/scigen/ (accessed April 04, 2012)
6. DBLP, http://www.informatik.uni-trier.de/~ley/db/ (accessed April 04, 2012)

Author Index